USING THE MACINTOSH COMPUTER AS A GRAPHIC DESIGN AND PRODUCTION TOOL

Desktop Design

BY LAURA LAMAR

WITH ILLUSTRATIONS BY

MAX SEABAUGH

CRISP PUBLICATIONS, INC.

LOS ALTOS, CALIFORNIA

Notes on Desktop Design
by Laura Lamar

Copyright © 1990,
by Crisp Publications, Inc.
All rights reserved.
No part of this publication may
be reproduced, stored in a
retrieval system, or transmitted,
in any form or by any
means, electronic, mechanical,
photocopying, recording,
or otherwise, without
the prior written permission
of the publisher.
For further information, write to
Crisp Publications, Inc.,
95 First Street,
Los Altos, California 94022.

Library of Congress Cataloging-in-Publication Data

Lamar, Laura.
   Notes on desktop design: using the Macintosh computer as a graphic design and production
tool / by Laura Lamar; with illustrations by Max Seabaugh. — 1st ed.
      p.   cm.
   ISBN 1-56052-001-9: $7.95
   1. Desktop publishing — Style manuals. 2. Printing, Practical-Layout — Data processing. I.
Title. II. Title: Desktop design.
Z286.D47L34   1989
686.2′2544 — dc20
                                                                89-81517
                                                                CIP

Dedication and Acknowledgments

*To Max, my husband and partner in all things,
with love.*

*To Mom and Dad, who gave me Art and Science,
with love, respect, and gratitude.*

*To Changhwan Kim, for his unfailing support and
assistance throughout this project.*

*Thanks to Apple Computer, Inc., The Compage
Company, and Letraset, USA, for getting me started
on the computer—and for keeping me going.*

*And special thanks to my students at the California
College of Arts and Crafts in San Francisco, for
using and testing this book in the classroom, and for
their many helpful suggestions.*

PREFACE

Graphic design is a fairly recent career option: when I attended school it was unknown. Anyone like me who loved to draw pictures and make handmade books thought perhaps they'd grow up to become an illustrator or commercial artist—at the time, the only words I knew to describe what I did. ■ I remember that one day when I was in high school, my mother, a painter, brought home a *Graphis* magazine from a New York shopping trip, saying, "Isn't *this* what *you* like to do?" I'll never forget it; in fact, I still have it. It was a special issue on Milton Glaser and Push Pin Studios, and it changed my life. Not because it showed me *what* to do—I already knew what that was going to be— but because it gave me a name for it, access to it, and heroes to emulate. ■ My path to becoming a graphic designer wasn't always direct, but I was lucky and eventually I became what I wanted to be. In the years since, I've tried to pay back that luck by lecturing, career counseling, and eventually, by teaching. ■ After I had taught typographic design to graphic design students at the California College of Arts and Crafts in San Francisco, California, for almost eight years, and had been a "conventional" graphic designer for almost twenty years, something important happened: I started using a Macintosh computer. This seemingly simple little machine changed the way I worked, and changed the tools and materials that I use. ■ I specialize in publication design; my primary medium is type. Before the Macintosh, I could never get my hands on type directly; I'd spec it, send it to a typesetter, and hope for the best. Now type is accessible; I can play with it, manipulate it, experiment with it. Words and design are more integrated. I find that I'm more adventurous, more productive. I've started writing, and, for the first time since I was a child, making my own books again—this is one. ■ Now I teach my students how to use the Macintosh as a design tool. This book was written for those students in response to the current lack of books on computer use for the typographically sophisticated but electronically uninitiated student. I hope it will help demystify the computer for you, too.

Laura Lamar
San Francisco, 1990

Contents

INTRODUCTION

This book is intended for graphic design students and professionals who already know the vocabulary and working methods of the design profession, but who are just learning to use a computer for the first time. We won't waste your time defining typographic or production terms—we assume you already know them. We won't waste space telling you how to set up your Macintosh—that information is already well covered in the *User's Guide* and other documentation that came with your computer. ■ So let's assume that you've purchased and set up your computer, and are ready to learn how to use it. Perhaps you've even bought some software already. Most Macintosh software programs share certain similarities; once you've learned the basics of one program, it becomes easier to learn another program. No matter what software you eventually intend to use, it won't hurt to master the basic vocabulary of the Macintosh environment and to understand a little about how the computer works. ■ The first part of this book—chapters one through five—will introduce you to the history of desktop publishing and its specific jargon, give you an overview of the hardware you'll encounter, explain the electronic environment you'll be working in and what software is and how you'll use it to accomplish specific design and production tasks on the Mac. ■ The second part of this book—chapters six through ten—will introduce you to a selection of software programs that cover the range of writing, drawing, and layout tasks you need to know as a designer, and will explain how to deal with type fonts and printing technology in this strange new world. ■ The information covered in this book will give you a broad overview and will hopefully answer the basic questions you'll have as you learn to use this new tool. Once you've learned the basics covered here, you'll be ready to go on by yourself and learn new software applications on your own. Most user's manuals contain good tutorials—chapters designed to walk you through a new program step by step—so you can teach yourself. Use them. If you have trouble, try looking up the answer in the manual by using the index, ask a friend, or call the technical support number provided. Finally, consider joining a local Macintosh users' group: there are hundreds throughout the country, and they provide technical support phone lines, special interest groups, and other ways for you to continue your learning. ■

Chapter 1: Desktop Publishing

Desktop publishing was a catchy phrase coined to describe a new way of doing an age-old task: setting type and producing page mechanicals— electronically. Today the term *desktop publishing* is passing out of favor with professionals as the new technology is increasingly accepted as just another publishing tool. Using the computer as a design tool doesn't necessarily imply that you'll forgo traditional printing of the final product, but it does imply that all or most of what is called "pre-press" work can be done using the Macintosh and a selection of electronic page design software products.

Illustration by Max Seabaugh in SuperPaint

COMPUTER-AIDED DESIGN

The design office of tomorrow, today: efficient, cost-effective, and productive

Illustration by Max Seabaugh in Adobe Illustrator; courtesy of Apple Computer, Inc.

Computers as a design aid

If *desktop publishing* doesn't fully describe using the computer as a design tool, what does? There isn't yet another widely accepted term, but some computer users are beginning to borrow a phrase from another field. The term *Computer-Aided Design* (CAD), originally used to describe engineering and architectural software programs, also appropriately describes the role of the computer within the graphic design industry.

The computer offers a new world of tools and technology with which to solve traditional design and production problems. It is possible to take a print production job from sketches to final camera-ready art on a computer, or to use the computer for any portion of a job, from sketching and visualizing, to preparation of comps, to illustration, chart, graph, and map-making, to typesetting and electronic page makeup. The work that you create in the initial stages of a project is carried through to the end, allowing you to work on, and refine, one "file." The once separate steps can now be one seamless flow from concept to finished product.

Computers can also help you to run your graphic design business by enabling you to prepare professional-looking slide presentations, written proposals, and invoices, and by helping you manage databases and mailing lists. Sophisticated spreadsheet and project management software can help you track expenses and time, coordinate progress reports, and do record-keeping and billings. And you can turn numbers into easily understood pictorial graphs to analyze how your business is doing and where it is heading.

Computers will never replace trained design professionals, because you, not the computer, are the true problem solver. But the computer is a powerful and versatile tool that can help you accomplish the business of design in a more efficient, cost-effective and productive manner.

A HISTORY OF DTP

A (very short) history

Desktop publishing is so new that it has hardly had time to *have* a history—but it has certainly *made* history. Johann Gutenberg—who is popularly credited with inventing movable type around 1440—would surely look with pleasure on this new technology that puts the power of the press into the reach of everyman.

Metal type

From Gutenberg's time until the mid-1800s, all typesetting was

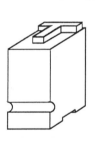

Metal type

done by hand with movable cast metal type. It was a highly skilled, time-consuming craft: metal type was painstakingly punched, then cast by hand. Books and other printed materials were scarce and valuable, although far more common than they were when they were hand-copied by monks and available only to a select few.

Automated typecasting

It was not until 1884 that the first successful automated type-casting machine was developed by Ottmar Mergenthaler; it enabled an operator to cast an entire line of type at once simply by operating a keyboard.

The auto-casting Linotype and Monotype machines, together with hand-set type, dominated typesetting until 1950, when the first phototypesetting machine was introduced by Intertype.

Photo and digital type

Today, photo-typesetting has virtually re-placed cast type because of its speed, versatility, and low cost. Digital typeset-ting entered the scene in the 1960s, and now

A digital letterform

coexists with phototypesetting as the standard means of setting type. Digital type describes letterforms—on computer type-setting equipment—as a series of very fine dots (greatly exag-gerrated in the illustration above) that are almost imper-ceptible to the naked eye.

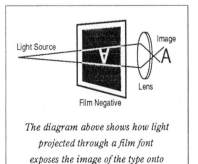

The diagram above shows how light projected through a film font exposes the image of the type onto light-sensitive paper or film.

Enter DTP

Desktop publishing—a phrase attributed to Paul Brainard of Aldus, a computer software company, and coined in 1985—is revolutionary because it puts the ability to set type into the hands of anyone willing to learn to use the new tool. And the tool is almost as simple to use as a typewriter—no longer the exclu-sive domain of skilled craftsmen like punchcutters or computer programmers.

The user friendly Macintosh interface designed by Apple Computer allows the computer user to "speak" to the computer using common English-language phrases, instead of complex computer program-ming language, making it possible for the average person to learn to use the computer without having to learn much about how the computer works.

PostScript language

In 1984, Apple Computer intro-duced the first Macintosh computer—an impressive improvement over its previous Apple and Lisa computers.

Illustrations by Cynthia Berglund in SuperPaint; courtesy of Apple Computer, Inc.

Letters are symbols that turn matter into spirit.

Alphonse de Lamartine, "Cours familier de litterature," Volume 6 Paris, 1858

Machines exist; let us then exploit them to create beauty— a modern beauty, while we are about it. For we live in the twentieth century; let us frankly admit it and not pretend that we live in the fifteenth.

Aldous Huxley, "Printing of Today," London, 1928

Shortly thereafter, Adobe Systems, a computer software company, introduced a programming language called PostScript that made it possible to reproduce high-quality images, including accurate reproductions of traditional typefaces. The PostScript language describes objects in mathematical terms, much like a combination of matrices and dots, or like lines drawn with a French curve.

Typefaces and illustrations described in PostScript can be rescaled and redrawn in any size, and can be sent to any PostScript-driven printer, such as a LaserWriter (a low-cost printer that you might have in your office or school), or to a Linotronic or Compugraphic typesetting machine (a high-end, expensive printer that your local typesetter or service bureau probably uses) for output.

Hand craftsmanship will never go out of usefulness in the graphic design profession, but it will be joined by computer craftsmanship as a marketable skill for the future.

The combination of the Macintosh computer, with its user-friendly interface, the PostScript programming language, and software applications and peripheral hardware from third-party developers (more about these in Chapters 3 and 5) quickly moved the Macintosh from the realm of hobbyist's toy to professional tool.

Its place?

Computer-aided design has not yet—and perhaps never will— entirely replace conventional typesetting. Although the gap is narrowing in the quality and variety of typography available, there will always be a place for fine typography and skilled craftsmanship. But there is also a tremendous use for this new

technology: from small-scale publishing of reports and newsletters by nonprofessionals, to comps and even finished artwork by design and publishing professionals.

Advantages of CAD

The economy and accessibility of type are the main advantages of using the computer as a design tool. Comps can be produced with "real" type and copy instead of "greeking," design, layout, and mechanicals can become one and the same electronic file, and can be done in fewer steps with actual copy

Illustration above by Max Seabaugh in Adobe Illustrator, courtesy of Apple Computer, Inc.; and opposite by Max Seabaugh in SuperPaint, courtesy of Macworld magazine.

and graphic elements. Electronic art can be reproduced, scaled, and altered with no stats and no whiteout. Proof prints for clients look much like the finished piece will, making corrections and alterations easier to catch and more economical to do.

Output quality

Low-cost PostScript printers such as the LaserWriter, and PostScript compatibility with high-end typesetting equipment, such as the Linotronic and Compugraphic typesetting machines, make it possible to produce professional typeset-quality output for proofing and pasteup. Links to high-end color separation systems such as Scitex, Crossfield, and Hell allow final output to take the form of separated, composite film negatives, ready for the printer to make into plates.

Disadvantages?

Once the design professional sent speced manuscripts to a professional typesetter, and sent artwork to a professional color separator—and relied on their expertise to do the job right. Today's computer user is left all alone, suddenly responsible for areas of expertise in which he may have no training. Not all designers want to become typesetters or separators, and rightly so. Such division of labor still ensures that qualified people take responsibility for

every aspect of the professional job. In computer-aided design, the temptation to do it all yourself—whether you're a designer, an editor, or a writer—is rife, and the true professional should *still* know when to stop doing it himself and pass the job along to a skilled subcontractor.

The temptation, too, to use this seductive new medium as the solution to *every* problem is just as dangerous. Remember always that the computer, like the pencil, is just a tool. In this case, a very sophisticated tool, but not always the right one for

every job. You, as the designer, are responsible for deciding what tool to use, and when.

Usefulness and advances

Today an increasing number of design offices and small businesses, corporate art departments, and publications are finding the speed, versatility, visualizing capabilities, and economy of the Macintosh useful in their work.

The enthusiasm—and criticism—of the design community will continually help make this tool better and bring it closer to our highest standards.

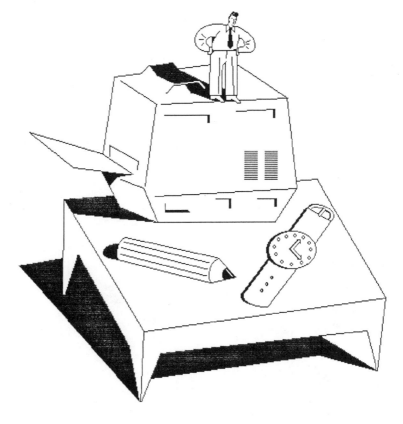

Visualization, economy, accuracy, and speed—four common reasons why computer-aided design is increasing in popularity.

THE PROCESS

1 Input When you work on a computer, you are working in an electronic environment. Hard copy elements—manuscripts or artwork on paper—must be brought (input) into that electronic environment before they can be manipulated on the computer. Copy is input by either typing it in on a keyboard, or importing it (opening it up) from a floppy disk on which previously keyboarded copy has been saved. Artwork and photographs are imported from files saved on floppy disks, or by scanning on a scanner or video digitizer.

2 Rough proofs & changes After the artwork and copy have been imported and worked with, rough page proofs are printed on proof-quality printers in order to make changes and corrections. Comps can be made using LaserWriter output.

3 Final proofs & approvals Proof prints are shown to proof-readers, clients, and others involved in the approval process. When all final corrections have been made, the files are ready to be output (printed out).

4 Output Files are sent to a service bureau electronically or on a floppy disk, where final prints can be output from a type-setting machine in negative or positive form on repro paper or film for use in pasteup or for sending to the printer.

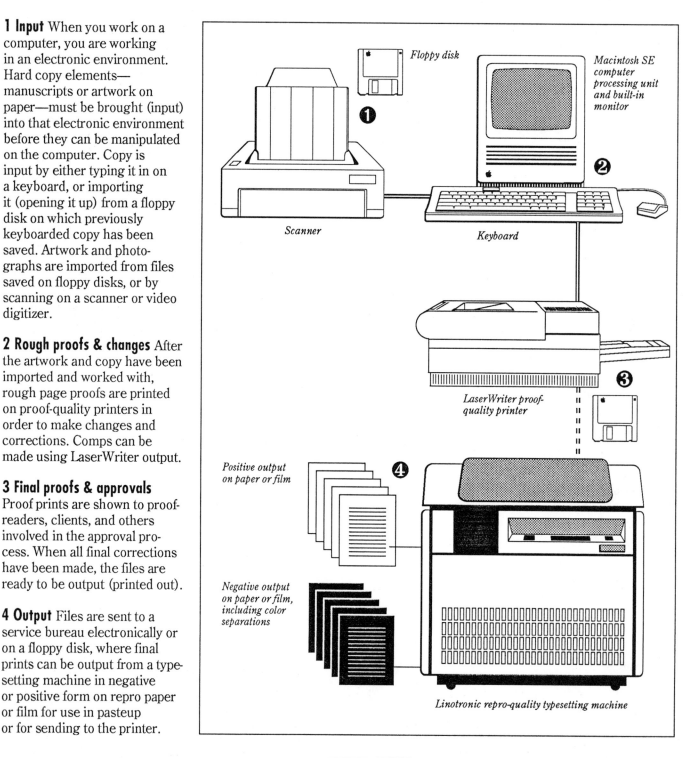

Floppy disk

Macintosh SE computer processing unit and built-in monitor

Scanner

Keyboard

LaserWriter proof-quality printer

Positive output on paper or film

Negative output on paper or film, including color separations

Linotronic repro-quality typesetting machine

Chapter 2: Vocabulary

Every field or specialty has its own jargon, or specific language. Related fields often share words or phrases, sometimes with identical meanings, sometimes with slightly different shadings of meaning. The language used in the Macintosh environment stems from the jargon of several different fields: computer science, printing, typography, and graphic design, among others. Sometimes when you hear a familiar-sounding word used within the context of the Macintosh world you may think you know what it means. Often, however, it has a unique, specific meaning in this context; it is this vocabulary that is the subject of this chapter.

Illustration by Max Seabaugh in Adobe Illustrator

MACINTOSH AS A FOREIGN LANGUAGE

Note: Italicized words appear in the Illustrated Dictionary starting on page 11.

The user interface

Part of the popularity of the Macintosh is that it was one of the first reasonably powerful personal computers to use sophisticated *software* programs to produce professional-quality work. But even more importantly, Apple Computer created a *user interface* that made the Macintosh easy to learn to use.

In the past, using a computer required lengthy training in a programming language in order to speak to the computer in "computer-eze." Apple decided to build in a combination of an English-language translator (or whatever language used by the computer user), and a pictorial symbol-based screen interface, enabling the computer user to speak to the computer in common English and by pointing to pictorial *icons*.

Using the vocabulary

Even with this user-friendly interface, there is still an entire language of specific computer jargon—essentially, a foreign language—that you should know in order to fully utilize the power of the Macintosh. The following text describes the basics of how the Macintosh system works, using many key words in context. For a more complete definition of any of the italicized words, see the Illustrated Dictionary starting on page 11 of this chapter.

The hardware configuration

The computer itself is just one part of what is called a *hardware* configuration—which includes the computer and other *peripheral devices*, or separate but connected pieces of hardware—that work together.

The CPU The *computer processing unit*, or CPU, is at the center of the configuration. The *user* (the person who works on the computer) interfaces with (talks to) the computer via several different kinds of *input devices*: data and instructions to the computer can be typed in on a typewriter-like *keyboard*, or *selected* using a small, handheld device called a *mouse* that's used to point to *commands* or pictorial *icons* on the *screen*.

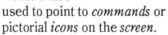

The monitor The *screen*, or monitor, allows the user to view work on a TV-like screen, which can be either built-in, like the screens shown on the Macintosh SE computers above, or can be separate peripherals, like the Radius screen shown here, which you attach to your computer via *cabling*. Monitors can be black and white only or full color, depending on the CPU you are using.

Storage devices

The work that is created on the computer is stored on magnetic storage devices called *disks*, somewhat like a cross between a cassette tape and a compact disk. Pocket-sized disks are called *floppy disks* and can store from 400 to 800 kilobytes (400k to 800k) of data—enough for hundreds of pages of *documents*. Large disks are called *hard disks* and commonly contain 20 to 80 megabytes (20MB, 80MB) of information or more.

Floppy disks are usually used to store the work that you, the user, create and save. They are also the medium on which the *software* programs and type *fonts* that you purchase are distributed by their manufacturers. When you purchase a floppy disk containing software, you can either run the software by inserting that floppy disk directly into your computer, or, more commonly, you can copy the program from the floppy and "load it" onto your hard disk. You work from the copy on your hard disk, saving the original floppy disk in a safe place as a *backup*.

Disk drives When you insert a floppy disk into your computer, you put it into a slot in the *disk drive*. Disk drives "read from" and "write to" disks. They can be built in, as shown in the pictures of the SE computers, left (they're the little slots in the middle of the face of the computer), or they can be separately attached peripherals, as shown here.

The HFS The hard disk becomes your file cabinet, in which you store your fonts and programs. In order to keep things organized, you use a *hierarchical filing system* (HFS), which allows you to create and name file *folders* in which to store the contents of your hard disk (or floppy disk). It is common practice to set up your hard disk with separate file folders in which to store different software programs for drawing, page layout, writing, and record-keeping.

The Desktop

When you turn on your computer, the first thing that you see onscreen is an area called the *Desktop*. The Desktop is a visual metaphor for your

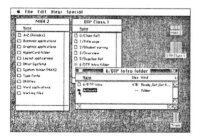

desk—it has a gray background like a desk blotter; there is an icon representing your "file cabinet" or hard disk, if you are using one; and there is even an icon for your trash can, if you want to throw something away.

Double-clicking to open Whenever you start work on the computer, you always start at the desktop. Then you open your "file cabinet," or hard disk, by pointing at it with the mouse-directed *pointer* (selection arrow) on the screen, and clicking twice (*double-clicking*) with the button on the top of the mouse. When the hard disk is open, a *directory window*

appears that displays all of the file folders stored on that hard disk. To open any file folder, you point to it with the mouse pointer, or selection arrow, and double-click. When you find the software program that you wish to use, you again use the mouse to double-click on the icon representing the program in order to open it.

Commands and tool icons Once you are "inside" a software program, you use the Macintosh *user interface* of pull-down

menus which list *selections* of *commands*, or instructions that you *select*—by clicking once with the pointer—in order to tell the computer what you want it to do. When a command is selected, it is *highlighted*. You can also select from a variety of *tool* icons such as pencils, erasers, spray-paint cans and paint buckets, scissors and magnifying glasses—all of which are used much like their real-life counterparts.

Windows Whenever you start new work in a software program, you begin by viewing an empty, untitled *window*. You always view your work through windows, and there are several different types of windows: directory windows, which list the contents of file folders or disks; document windows, which display the work that you are creating within a software

The Macintosh is easy to learn to use because you can give the computer instructions simply by pointing to a command on a pull-down menu. When you become more expert at using a particular software program, you can begin to use keyboard short-cuts for some commands. Keyboard short-cuts, when available, always appear to the right of a command on the pull-down menu, so you can memorize them or look them up by glancing at the pull-down menu. Keyboard short-cuts save you time by allowing you to "mouse" with one hand, and type in commands with the other.

One of the great strengths of working electronically can also be a weakness: electronic files are quickly and easily copied, moved—and deleted or damaged. Learn to save your work often—every 15 minutes is a good rule of thumb, or after the minimum amount of time that you'd be willing to spend recreating lost data. Make backups frequently, too. Backups are not the same as saves: they are separate, duplicate copies of your files, saved onto other, separate disks. Backups not only protect you in case your work is lost due to an accident such as a power failure, they also give you the opportunity to go back and work on an earlier version of a file.

program; and *dialog boxes*, little windows in which the computer talks to you, to ask you questions or to let you make choices about the work that you are doing.

Viewing If what you are working on is too big to be seen all at once through the *window*, you can grab the work itself— like a sheet of paper—with a "hand icon" and slide it around behind the window until you bring the covered-up portion of the work, or document, into view. Or, you can resize the window so that it better displays the work it contains, or change the viewing scale using a magnifying/reducing glass icon, making the work in the window appear larger or smaller so that it can be seen better.

Saving and re-opening When you are ready to *save* the work that you have done, you give your *document* a name, so that both you and your computer can identify it later. Then you tell the computer which disk you

want to store the document on, and instruct the computer to save the *file* to that disk. Later,

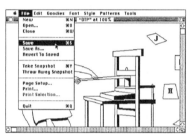

you can re-open the document by double-clicking directly on the icon (or name) representing that document. As long as the

software program originally used to create that document is loaded, or filed, on your hard disk, the document will automatically open up within its parent program. You can make changes to your document at any time, and save the changes—or change your mind, and decide not to save the changes.

Duplicating and copying You can make copies of your document onto another floppy disk or hard disk, using the same name. But if you want to make another copy (or copies) of a document on the same disk, you must give it a new name. Commonly, a numbered variant of the original name is used: Document, Document.2,

Document.3, etc. Numbered variations like this are frequently used when a series of revisions to an original file is planned, helping you date the changes and keep track of the order in which the copies were made.

Software

Software, program, and *application* are all somewhat interchangeable terms for the programming tools that you use on your computer to create documents. Different kinds of software programs are specialists in different kinds of tasks: some help you to create written materials, and are called word processing programs. Others help you to create drawings and pictures, and these are called graphics programs. Still others help you set type and create page layouts, and these are called page layout programs. There are many kinds of software for the Macintosh, but they all share a similar user interface of pull-down menus, tools, and icons, so that once you learn to use one or two programs, it becomes easier to learn to use a new one.

The next chapters will tell you more about hardware, the desktop, and software, and teach you how to use several popular basic software programs in each category.

AN ILLUSTRATED DICTIONARY

Activate: To cause a *command* or an action to take place (see *mouse*).

Apple key: See *Command key*.

Application, program, software: A type of *software* program that enables you to create documents and do specific kinds of tasks that manipulate objects or information. Usually called either application or program. For example, graphics programs are for drawing pictures, word processing programs help you to write and edit manuscripts, spreadsheet programs help you to process numerical data, and page layout programs help you to design and lay out pages and to spec type. Many other kinds of specialized programs exist.

Backup: Making extra copies of *files, documents,* or *disks* for safety. When you first purchase software, you make a copy of the contents of the disk by copying it onto another disk, called a backup disk. When you save files and documents, it's a good idea to make more than one copy; if anything should happen to your original, you can always fall back on your backup.

Beta software: *Software* that is still undergoing development and testing; pre-release software (not on the market yet). Frequently distributed to beta test sites—specially chosen firms or individuals who can try out and evaluate the new software—for testing.

Bomb: A system or *software* failure that causes the program to crash, or cease functioning. Requires rebooting (restarting) the computer. Usually caused by software incompatibilities or *bugs*.

Boot: To start the computer up; to turn it on.

Bug: A flaw in the *software* or *application* that causes it to behave improperly or erratically. Not the same as a *virus*, which is a self-replicating, invasive programming code that can destroy system files.

Cabling: Insulated wires that connect *peripheral devices* to the *computer processing unit,* or to one another.

Click: To position the *mouse*-directed *pointer* (or *selection*) arrow on something on the *screen*, then press and quickly release the *mouse button*. A technique used to *select* (*highlight*) *objects* on the screen.

Click and drag: To position the *pointer* on something onscreen, then, still holding the *mouse button* down, *drag* the selected *object* by moving the *mouse*. Used to move objects and to resize objects and *windows*.

Command: A word or phrase that describes an action for the computer to perform. Commands appear under pull-down *menus* in the menu bar, which, when *selected*, become *highlighted*. Or a command can be entered by typing command equivalents on the *keyboard;* these are called keyboard shortcuts. Keyboard command equivalents, when available, appear on the pull-down menus to the right of the command name. Keyboard shortcuts can sometimes be quicker than using the pull-down menu commands. Knowing how to use both kinds of commands is the most efficient approach.

Italicized words can be found elsewhere as separate entries in this Illustrated Dictionary. Cross-referencing listings will help you to fully understand each single definition.

The bomb icon signifies a program or system crash

Cabling wires connect your printer, scanner, and other peripheral devices to your computer

A pull-down menu showing a command highlighted and with keyboard equivalents to the right of some commands

The Command key

Command key: A key that, when held down while another key is pressed or a *mouse* action is performed, causes a *command* to take effect. Also sometimes called the Apple key (or, to PC users, the Control key). It's located in slightly different positons on different keyboards, but is always in the lower left corner of the keyboard, and has an Apple logo and a pretzel-like *icon* on its face.

Computer unit (CPU)

Computer; central processing unit (CPU): The basic piece of *hardware*, encased in a rigid plastic box, that contains the central processing unit necessary to run *software applications* and do computing tasks. Macintosh personal computers are compact, all-in-one units that sometimes also contain an internal *hard disk* for storage, a *disk drive*, and a built-in *screen*.

Control panel: A *desk accessory* found under the Apple menu that lets you specify computer preferences such as *mouse* and *keyboard* speeds, *desktop* background patterns, speaker volume, and so on.

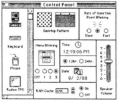

Control panel dialog box

Current startup disk: The startup *disk* on whose system files the Macintosh is currently running. The startup disk is installed on your *hard disk*, if you have one, or you can also *boot* from a system on a *floppy disk*. The startup disk must have a System folder that is activated, i.e., that contains a System, a Finder, and the several other files necessary for the Macintosh to run itself. The computer can only run on one system at a time, so be careful to have only one active system available to it at a time. You can test if a system folder is activated by *selecting* the View by Icon *command* from the View menu on the *Desktop*; if active, a small *icon* of a Macintosh will appear within the System folder icon.

Desk accessories, DAs: Mini-*applications* found under the Apple *menu* that can be used while you're inside another regular application. Examples are the alarm clock, calculator, key caps, note pad, and camera. DAs do small, limited tasks, not always found in applications, that are useful additions to them, like writing notes, looking up where font symbols appear on the keyboard, setting an alarm clock, or pasting pictures into a "scrapbook" for future use.

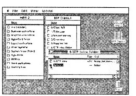

The Desktop

Desktop: "Home base" on the Macintosh: the first thing that you see when you turn on the computer and the place you exit from when you turn off the computer. Also the place from which you enter into all *applications*, and the place that you return to when you exit, or quit, an application. Also the place where you can review the *directories* of the contents of *disks* and *folders*, create and name new folders, move and rename *files* and folders, and duplicate the contents of files, folders, or disks. See also *Finder*.

Dialog box: A box, or *window*, that contains a message from the computer, requesting more information from you, asking you to *select* an option, or giving you a message about the current function.

Dimmed command: A *command* in a pull-down *menu* that is grayed-back. A dimmed command means that that choice is not currently available to you; perhaps because another function needs to be accomplished before that *selection* can be made. For example, the Font menu and commands will appear dimmed until you use the *I-beam tool* to select an area of type for the command to be applied to.

Dimmed icon: A grayed-back *icon* indicates that the object it represents, such as a *disk*, or a *folder* or *document* on a disk, has either been opened (in which case a *directory window* of its contents should be visible on the *Desktop*) or been ejected from the *disk drive*. If a floppy disk has been ejected, just reinsert it into any disk drive to open it and work on its contents. It is possible to eject a floppy disk (using Command-E) and still view the contents of its directory in order to move or copy files or folders from the ejected disk to a disk currently inside the disk drive. The computer will ask you to insert or eject each disk as necessary while it completes the copying process, a procedure known as "disk swapping."

A dimmed folder icon

Directory or directory window: A box, or *window*, containing a list of the contents of a *disk* or *folder*. The contents can be listed (viewed) pictorially, alphabetically, or by size, date, or kind. To change viewing mode, go to the View *menu* on the *Desktop* and *select* a new viewing mode *command*.

A directory window

Disk: The magnetic medium on which the computer stores information. Macintosh computers use portable 3.5" *floppy disks* or larger *hard disks* (which can be either built-in or external *peripheral devices*), or both, to store data on.

Disk drive: The *hardware* unit or mechanism that holds the *disk*, "reads" information off it, and "writes" (*saves*) information onto it. A *hard disk* drive has both the disk and the reading mechanism permanently encased inside it. A *floppy disk* drive requires that you insert a portable 3.5" floppy disk into it. Both floppy and hard disk drives can be internal (built into the CPU) or external (not built-in, separate, *peripheral*).

A 3.5" floppy disk

Document: A *file*; whatever you create with an *application* on the Macintosh; information you enter, modify, view, or *save*, such as copy written in a word-processing program, or a drawing made with a graphics application. Documents can be one or many pages in length, but a document is only one electronic file. Each document, or file, that is created and saved has its own identifying name.

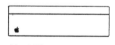
A hard disk

Documentation: The written materials, such as the users manuals, guides, or quick reference cards, that come with a *software* program and explain its functions and how to use them.

A floppy disk drive

Double-click: To position the *mouse*-directed *pointer* (or *selection*) arrow on the *screen* where you want an action to take place, and then press and release the *mouse button* twice in quick succession without moving the mouse. The first click selects the object and the second click opens it. A technique used to *select* and open *documents*, *files*, and *application icons*. In addition, it is a handy shortcut in many programs for selecting type (it doesn't, however, work in all programs): insert your *I-beam tool* anywhere in a word and click twice: the whole word will automatically be selected without dragging across it. In some applications, if you click three times, that whole line of type will be selected, and four times selects the whole paragraph.

Drag: To position the *mouse*-driven *pointer* on or near something on the *screen*, press and hold down the *mouse button*, move the mouse, and then release the mouse button. A technique used in moving and *selecting* large *objects* and groups of objects, and in selecting areas of text. See also *click and drag*.

A file or document icon

File: Generic term for a collection of information stored on a *disk*, such as a *document*, a system file such as the *System* or *Finder*, an *application*, etc.

Finder: An *application* that's always available on the *Desktop*, but invisible to you as you use it. You use it automatically when you manage *documents* and *applications*, and when you get information from (read) or *save* information (write) to a *disk*. It's also what enables you to create and name *files* and *folders* at the Desktop level. You probably won't even be aware of the Finder when you're using it. When you're at the Desktop, you are also "at the Finder." When you are in an application and wish to return to the Finder or Desktop, save your work by selecting Save from the File menu, then choose Quit from the File menu and you will go back to the Desktop.

A folder icon

bB bB *bB bB*

The Bodoni font family, showing four fonts all in the same point size: Bodoni book, Bodoni bold, Bodoni book italic, and Bodoni bold italic

Floppy disk: A portable magnetic disk on which the computer stores information. Macintoshes use 3.5" rigid floppy disks.

Folder: Just like a manila folder on your desk, Macintosh folders hold *documents*, *applications*, or other folders—whatever you want to put into them. Folders allow you to organize *files* in any way you want. To create a new folder when you're at the *Desktop*, type Command-N. See also *hierarchical file system*.

Fonts: Conventionally, a term used to describe one specific point size and style of a type family, as in a metal type font; for example, 12 point Bodoni book. In the Macintosh environment, font has a broader meaning: because all type can be scaled to different sizes, font means an entire range of sizes of a particular style in a family of type; for example, Bodoni book in any point size. A font family would include all point sizes and all styles available; for example, Bodoni book, Bodoni bold, Bodoni book italic, and Bodoni bold italic. The Macintosh uses two kinds of fonts: *screen* fonts, which provide bit-mapped versions of the font for viewing that font onscreen, and printer fonts, which are files containing the *PostScript* descriptions of the fonts to send to the printer, or *output device*, for printing. Printer fonts are stored loose in the System folder; screen fonts are installed directly into the *System file* using the Font/DA Mover *utility*.

A hard disk

Hard disk: A storage device; a large capacity (usually 20MB or more) *disk* and reading mechanism permanently encased in a hard plastic casing; it can be built into the CPU or can be a separate *peripheral device*.

Hardware: The physical parts of a computer configuration, such as the computer itself, the printer, the *disk drive*, the screen, or scanner. Any part of the Macintosh configuration that you can touch.

by sharing information, su: insights with each other. This is an intentionally **Apple User Groups** exist fr Apple has ever made, and application in which these

Highlighted text

Hierarchical file system (HFS): A feature that lets you nest *files* and *folders* within other folders, to create as many levels in a hierarchy as you need to organize your information. Opening a folder to display its *directory* shows only the information within that folder, so that you don't have to clutter your *Desktop*.

Highlight: To *select* something, such as an *icon* or an *object*, by *clicking* on it with the *pointer*, or selection arrow. When a *disk* or *folder icon* is selected, it will turn gray or black. When an object is selected, it will appear with little black boxes (handles) around it. Text is selected by clicking and dragging the *I-beam tool* across it. Highlighted text is indicated by turning the word, line, or paragraph black.

I-beam tool: A *tool* used for *selecting,* entering, or *highlighting* text. When text is highlighted by *clicking and dragging* with this tool it turns black. When you click with the tool inside a line of type, a blinking "insertion bar," or vertical line, will appear. Whatever you type will be inserted after, or to the right of, a blinking insertion bar. To delete text a character at a time, press the Delete key, and copy will be deleted one character at a time to the left of the insertion bar. To delete an entire line or block of text, select (highlight) the text with the *I-beam tool* and press the Delete key.

The I-beam tool

Icon: A graphic representation of an *object,* a concept, or a message, such as the *trash can* and *folder* images on the *Desktop.*

The trash can and folder icons

Initialize: To prepare a new *disk* to receive information; also used to erase used disks. To initialize a new *floppy disk,* insert it into the *disk drive* and *select* either single-sided (if you are using a Macintosh 512) or double-sided (if you are using a Macintosh Plus, SE, or II) in the *dialog box* that appears. When the process is finished, another dialog box will ask you to name the disk. To initialize either a floppy or a hard disk from the desktop, first select the disk *icon,* then choose Erase Disk from the Special *menu* on the *Finder.* **CAUTION:** Do not erase or initialize a disk until you are sure that there are no valuable *files* or *applications* on that disk. **NEVER** erase the *hard disk* icon installed on your computer: it contains all of your working applications and type *fonts.* See "To Turn Off the Mac" on page 36 in order to avoid making this mistake.

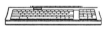
A mouse

Input devices: *Peripheral hardware* such as the *keyboard* or *mouse* that is used to enter data, *selections,* or *commands* into the computer.

Keyboard: The typewriter-like *input device* used for typing in data (words and numbers) and *commands.*

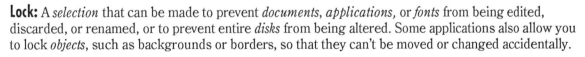
A keyboard

Lock: A *selection* that can be made to prevent *documents, applications,* or *fonts* from being edited, discarded, or renamed, or to prevent entire *disks* from being altered. Some applications also allow you to lock *objects,* such as backgrounds or borders, so that they can't be moved or changed accidentally.

Some programs allow you to lock and unlock objects in a dialog box. At the desktop level, you can lock a file by selecting it with the pointer, typing Command-I to get an Information dialog box, and clicking an X in the lock box as shown here

Megabyte (MB): A unit of measurement equal to 1024 kilobytes. There are 400k (kilobytes) on a single-sided 3.5" *floppy disk,* and 800k on a double-sided floppy disk. *Hard disks* usually start at 20MB (megabytes) of storage, and go up to several hundred MB.

Memory: The place in the computer's main unit that temporarily stores information while you are working, before it is stored on a *hard disk* or a *floppy disk.* The Macintosh SE comes with at least 1 megabyte of memory you can use temporarily for your work (until you *save* it), and 256k of *ROM* that stores certain information that the computer needs to run itself. You can purchase, and have installed, extra memory in the form of 1MB chips. Memory and storage are not the same: consider memory to be temporary, enabling you to perform functions, and storage to be permanent, enabling you to save the work you have created. See also *storage devices, RAM* and *ROM.*

Menu with highlighted command

Menu, pull-down menu: A list of *commands* that appears when you *click* and hold down the *mouse button* while pointing to the menu title in the menu bar at the top of the screen. The menu bar is the horizontal strip at the top of the screen that contains menu titles. Notice that the menu bars in the *Finder*, and in different *applications*, contain some similar, and some different, menus. The menu title is the word or phrase in the menu bar that designates one menu. Pressing on the menu title causes the title to be *highlighted* and the pull-down menu to appear below it. To *select* a command from a pull-down menu, open the menu and *drag* down until the desired command is *highlighted*, then release the mouse button.

Modem: A *peripheral device* that links your Macintosh to a phone line, through which you can send or receive files over the telephone lines by calling a modem phone number directly, leaving a message in a "mailbox" on a network or electronic mail service, or by downloading (transferring) *files* from an electronic community "bulletin board."

A mouse; used with the cabling facing away from the user; the mouse button is at the top

Mouse: The small *peripheral device* (actually invented by the Xerox Corporation) connected to your computer by *cabling*, that you roll around on a flat surface next to your computer. When you move the mouse, a *pointer* arrow on the *screen* moves correspondingly. With the mouse, you can *select* objects and menu *commands* on the screen by pointing to them with the arrow, and activate the selection by *clicking*, *double-clicking*, or *dragging* the mouse.

Mouse button: The button on the top of the *mouse*. In general, pressing the mouse button initiates an action on whatever is underneath the *pointer*, and releasing the button confirms the action.

Object: A graphic object on the *screen* that has been created with an object *tool* such as a circle, square, or line tool, such as are found in graphics programs. Also, an object such as a picture block or a text block. See more about objects in Chapters 7 and 8.

Open: To *double-click* on an *icon*; this leads you to either a *window* containing a *directory* of contents (of a *disk* or *folder*), to an empty window or *dialog box* from which you can create a new *document*, or to a window containing a document that had previously been created in an *application* and *saved*.

A LaserWriter printer

Output device: Any printer or typesetting machine that can be connected to a computer, run by it, and on which you can print out on paper, typesetting paper, or film, a reproduction of your document. Data is sent to printers in *PostScript* or another programming language, depending on the software used to create the data. Quality of output is what is called "device independent," meaning that the same file can be printed on any printer, but the quality will vary according to the capabilities of the printer, not the file. Low-end printers, such as the dot-matrix or ImageWriter printers, output at 72 dots per inch (dpi) resolution. Medium-range LaserWriter printers output at 300 dpi. High-end Linotronic typesetting machines output at 1270 to 2540 dpi. Color printers (such as the QMS) output color pages in CMYK (short for cyan, magenta, yellow, and black, the four process printing colors) at 300 dpi, and are similar to a color copier in quality. Each brand or make of printer may vary in its dpi, or resolution.

A Linotronic typesetting machine

Peripheral device: A piece of computer *hardware*—such as a *disk drive*, printer (*output device*), *modem,* or monitor (*screen*)—used in conjunction with a computer and under the computer's control. Peripheral devices are usually separate from the computer, but connected to it by *cabling* that allows the computer to communicate with the device using programming languages such as *PostScript,* TrueType, or QuickDraw, via communications software such as Appletalk.

A trio of peripheral devices, left to right: an external floppy disk drive, a LaserWriter printer, and a full-page monitor.

Pixels, bits, rasters: The small square dots that you see onscreen that make up the *screen* image; the dots that print out when you use "bit-mapped" (pixelated) programs such as MacPaint and SuperPaint.

Pointer, selection arrow: A small shape on the *screen*, usually an arrow, that follows the movement of the *mouse*. Use the tip of the arrow to *select* an *icon* by *clicking* on it, or open an icon by *double-clicking* .

The pointer, or selection arrow

PostScript: A programming language developed by Adobe Systems, Inc., a software company that also creates and sells type *fonts* and graphics programs for the Macintosh. PostScript is a mathematical description of forms based on bezier curves; it essentially describes points along a french curve, and places that data on a matrix on the page. Data described in PostScript can be scaled, warped, manipulated, rotated, and printed at any size. It is especially useful for accurately reproducing the forms of type fonts and illustrative material, because PostScript objects print smooth, not pixellated,and the fineness of the image is limited only by the resolution of the *output device* on which the file is printed.

Printer, printing: See *Output device.*

RAM: An acronym for random-access memory, the part of the computer's *memory* that stores data temporarily while you're working on it. Information in RAM is temporary, and will be stored only until you *save* it to a *hard* or *floppy disk* (or *storage device*), or until the power goes off, either by turning off the computer intentionally, or through a malfunction or power surge. See also *memory* and *ROM.*

ROM: An acronym for read-only memory, the part of *memory* that contains information the computer uses (along with the system files) throughout the system, including the information it needs to get itself started. Information on ROM is permanent; it doesn't vanish when you switch the power off. It is not available to you as the user; it is used by the computer to run itself. The Macintosh SE comes with 256k of ROM. See also *memory* and *RAM.*

A Macintosh SE with built-in monitor

Save: A *command* found under the File menu that allows you to "write" (permanently save) information to a *disk*. In most (but not all) *applications*, the keyboard shortcut Command-S will also save. Until information that you create is saved, it is only temporary, and will disappear if you turn the computer off or lose power unexpectedly. It is very important to save frequently—a good rule of thumb is to save at the end of every page, at the end of every task sequence, or no less often than the amount of time you'd be willing to spend recreating lost data in the case of a power interruption.

A peripheral full-page monitor

Screen, monitor: A television-like screen on which you view the work, or *document*, that you are creating on the computer. A screen can be either built-in, or a separate *peripheral device* connected to the CPU by *cabling*. Small, 9" diagonal black and white screens are built in to the Macintosh Plus and SE models, or you can also purchase larger full- or two-page sized black and white peripheral screens. Mac II, IIcx, and IIci models, which can process and display color work, come with a 13" diagonal color monitor, or you can purchase even larger peripheral color screens manufactured by other companies.

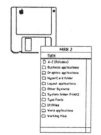

A vertical scroll bar from the right-hand side of a window, showing up and down scroll arrows, the moveable scroll box, and, at the bottom, the size box

Screen resolution: The "line screen" or number of dots (rasters) per inch (dpi) on a *screen* or monitor. Screen resolution can be as low as 72 dots per inch, similar to the resolution of the coarsest *output device*, the dot-matrix ImageWriter printer. Screen resolution has nothing to do with the resolution of the output device when you print your work—it is "device independent." See also *output device*.

Scroll: To move a *document* or *directory* in its *window* so that you can see a different part of it. The scroll bar is a narrow rectangular bar that can appear at the right and/or bottom of a window. *Clicking* in the gray section of a scroll bar causes the visible portion of the document to move in the direction indicated by your action. The scroll box inside the scroll bar indicates the position of what's in the window relative to the entire document page. *Dragging* the scroll box changes the view of the document. The scroll arrows, which appear at either end of a scroll bar, allow you to scroll in two ways: clicking a scroll arrow moves the document or directory one line at a time, in the direction that the arrow is pointing. Pressing a scroll arrow scrolls the document continuously. Scrolling is only available, if at all, in the currently active window, and then only if the window is sized smaller than the contents of the document or directory. Some *applications*—especially drawing programs—also have a hand or grabber *tool*, which allows you to "grab" the document and slide it around inside the window to change the view.

Select, selection: To designate where the next action will take place by *clicking* on *objects* (with the pointer arrow) or *dragging* across text (with the *I-beam tool*). Selected objects (selections) are *highlighted*. See also *highlight, I-beam tool*, and *pointer*.

Shift-click, group select: A technique that lets you make more than one *selection* at a time, by holding down the Shift key while you select something in addition to the current selection. The Shift key appears twice, once each on the lower left and right sides of the *keyboard*.

Size box: The box in the lower right corner of most active *windows* that lets you change the window shape and size by dragging it. Resizing windows allows you to fit several windows onscreen at once without obscuring information, and to change how much of a *document* you're able to view through the window at one time.

Software: *Applications*, programs, or instructions for the computer to carry out. The computer reads these instructions from *floppy disks* inserted into the *disk drive* or from a program installed on (copied onto) a *hard disk*.

Startup disk: A *floppy* or *hard disk* that contains the *system software* the computer needs to get itself started. A startup disk must contain an activated System folder, i.e., one that contains a *System file* and the *Finder*. It will probably contain several other files such as General, print resources such as LaserWriter and Laser Prep, *Keyboard* and *Mouse* files, and printer *fonts* and *desk accessories*. **IMPORTANT:** Be very careful not to confuse the computer by presenting it with two startup disks at once. It might try to "read" from both startup disks and get confused, circling back and forth between the two. If it's necessary, once the computer is running, to insert another disk that holds an activated System folder to get to a document, be very careful not to *select* the second system, or to start the *document* or

The System folder that runs your Macintosh can be on either a floppy disk, as shown here, or installed permanently on your hard disk.

application on that disk. Instead, to be extra-safe, copy the files you need onto your hard disk, or onto a floppy without a System folder. **NOTE:** Advanced users may use a variety of startup disks, with System files loaded with different selections of fonts and desk accessories needed for a particular job.

A surefire way to tell if a system folder is activated: at the Desktop, choose View by Icon from the Special menu. If a small Macintosh icon appears inside the system folder icon, the system is activated. If not, it cannot be used as a startup system.

Storage device: an electronic medium contained in a piece of hardware that holds data and applications permanently—or at least until they are erased. Floppy disks, hard disks, and external hard disks are all storage devices.

System file: the *file* the computer uses to start itself up, or to provide system-wide information. Although the System file is represented by an *icon*, it cannot be opened in the usual way by *double-clicking* on the icon. It can, however, be altered by the use of special *utilities* such as the Font/ DA Mover (which installs screen *fonts* and *desk accessories* in the system), or the Installer (which installs new versions of the System file and *Finder* in your startup system).

System software: the *files* and resources in the System folder that the computer uses to run itself, and to communicate to and from *peripheral devices* such as the *keyboard* and *mouse*, the printer (*output device*), or a large screen *monitor*.

Template: usually a MacPaint *file* created by scanning a sketch. Used as a background over which one can trace in programs such as Adobe Illustrator.

Some typical tools (these from SuperPaint). From left to right, top to bottom: the Magnifying glass, Lasso, Paintbrush, Pencil, Spraycan, Eraser, Paintbucket, and Type tools.

Tools: *icons* available in every *application* that enable you to perform specific tasks. The *pointer* (selection arrow) and *I-beam tool* are common to every program. Other specialized tools are also available, such as pencil, paintbrush, and eraser tools in drawing applications, *object* tools that create lines, circles, squares, and other graphic objects, and a variety of text and picture tools. Learning the basic tools in beginner's programs makes it easier to recognize and use more advanced tools in advanced programs. To use any tool, first *click* on the tool icon with the selection arrow to *select* it, then either use it directly on the page to create an object by *clicking and dragging*, or use it to select and manipulate an existing object.

The trash can icon is always found on the Desktop—and is, in fact, one way to tell that you are at the Desktop.

Trash can: an *icon* in the lower right corner of the *Desktop* that you use to discard *documents*, *folders*, and *applications*. When full, the trash can icon is swollen. When the trash is emptied, by selecting Empty Trash from the Special *menu*, it reverts to its normal width. The trash is emptied automatically whenever you start an application, eject a *floppy disk*, or when the *Finder* needs space for *memory*. To retrieve something from a full trash can, *double-click* on the trash icon to open a *window* with a directory of the contents of the trash. *Select* the desired object and *drag* it out of the trash can back to wherever you want to keep it. **SHORTCUT:** You can eject a disk quickly by dragging its icon to the trash— don't worry, it won't trash the disk, just eject it. This is, in fact, the most common way to eject disks. Bad metaphor; but a handy trick!

The Macintosh user interface combines two input devices—the mouse and the keyboard (above)—with pictorial icons and windows (below) as well as pull-down menus, English-language commands, and selectable pictorial tools.

This scrolling window has a close box in the upper left corner, a zoom box in the upper right corner, scroll bars and arrows at the right and bottom, and a size box in the lower right corner. Grabbing and dragging the gray bars at the top lets you move the window around on the Desktop

The wristwatch icon— or, in some programs, a rotating ball or other icon—indicates that the computer is busy processing your last command, and you should wait for it to finish before proceeding.

Clicking on the zoom box makes the currently selected window pop completely open; clicking a second time returns it to its original size, shape, and position.

User: The person using the computer. Computer how-to books are called user's guides or manuals.

User interface: The combination of *mouse, keyboard,* pictorial *icons* and *tools,* pull-down *menus, windows,* and English-language *commands* that make using the Macintosh easy to use, or "user friendly."

Utility program: A special-purpose *application* that allows you to open and alter *system software* or lets you perform some useful function on your files. Examples are the Font/DA Mover, which installs *fonts* and *desk accessories* into your *System file,* and the Installer, which installs new versions of the System and *Finder* onto your startup system.

Version: Whenever software is corrected and tiny flaws or *bugs* are fixed, it is re-released under an altered version number. Whenever a major revision of that software is released with new features (and usually new *documentation*), it is given a new version number. Examples would be Microsoft Word 1.5 and Microsoft Word 3.0. The former is a revised release of version 1.0; the latter is an entirely new version.

Virus: A self-replicating, invasive programming code that can damage or destroy *files* and *documents.* Anti-virus software programs are available that can detect the presence of a virus on a disk and, in some cases, remove or repair the damaged files. Not every anti-virus program can detect every virus, and new viruses appear frequently, so it is recommended that you keep up with the Macintosh news media reports on new viruses, and select your anti-virus programs carefully to try to protect yourself fully. Viruses can be a real menace, and cost you valuable work time and loss of files, so it is well worth your time to avoid contamination.

Window: The area that displays information on the *Desktop.* You view *documents* and *directories* through a window. You can open or close a window, change its size and shape, move it around on the Desktop (by grabbing it with the *selection* arrow on the gray-striped bars at its top, and *dragging* it), scroll through its contents (if it's a scrolling window), and edit its contents.

Wristwatch: An *icon* that you see on the *screen* when the computer is performing a function that causes you to wait. You cannot start another function until the wristwatch turns back into an arrow, or whatever *tool* you were using when the wristwatch icon appeared. Sometimes the hands on the watch will move, indicating that the action is being performed. Sometimes (depending on the application) the hands don't move. If it's taking a very long time, be patient. Some computing tasks do take a long time. But sometimes your computer appears to get stuck on the wristwatch, and this can be a sign of a malfunction. If you have access to an advisor or help line, ask them for assistance. It may be necessary to restart the computer by using a programmer's switch (see your User's Guide) or turning the power off and then on again quickly; but please, never do this without supervision or advice.

Zoom box: The small box in the upper right corner of the title bar of some *windows.* Clicking a zoom box expands the window to its maximum size; clicking it again returns the window to its former size.

Chapter 3: Hardware

Hardware is the word we use to describe the actual machines that constitute a computer configuration, or setup. In addition to the *CPU*, or main computer processing unit, a configuration will probably include a *hard disk*, or storage device, a *screen*, or viewing monitor, a printer, or *output device*, and a *keyboard* and *mouse*, or *input devices*. It might also include a few extras such as a scanner or video digitizer, for inputting photos, sketches, or typewritten copy, or a *modem* for linking up with other computers or information services via the telephone lines.

Illustration by Max Seabaugh in Adobe Illustrator

ANATOMY OF A MACINTOSH

A Macintosh SE, with a standard keyboard and mouse

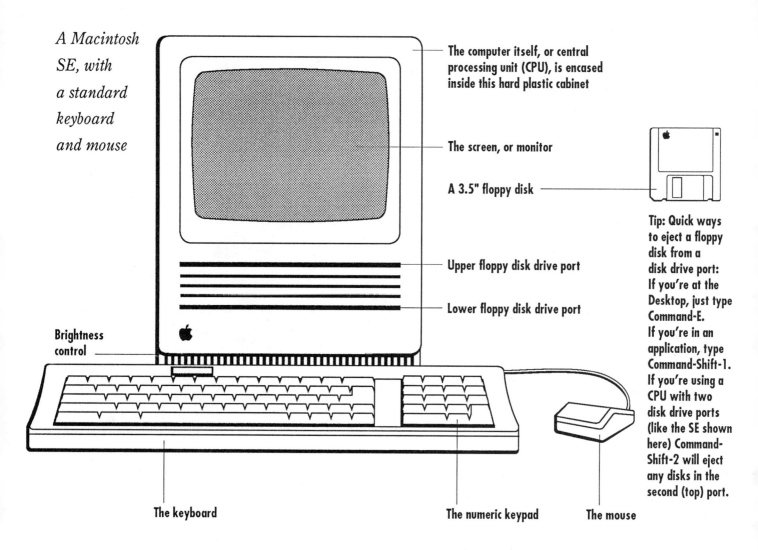

The computer itself, or central processing unit (CPU), is encased inside this hard plastic cabinet

The screen, or monitor

A 3.5" floppy disk

Upper floppy disk drive port

Lower floppy disk drive port

Brightness control

The keyboard

The numeric keypad

The mouse

Tip: Quick ways to eject a floppy disk from a disk drive port: If you're at the Desktop, just type Command-E. If you're in an application, type Command-Shift-1. If you're using a CPU with two disk drive ports (like the SE shown here) Command-Shift-2 will eject any disks in the second (top) port.

Definitions of italicized words can be found in the Illustrated Dictionary on pages 11 through 20.

A Macintosh SE, the "basic" model (shown above), is a simple-looking machine. The computer and *screen*, or monitor, are housed in one piece of *hardware*, and the *mouse* and *keyboard* are attached to it with *cabling*. Both the keyboard and mouse are *input devices*, which you use to enter information or *selections* into the computer. The screen displays only a portion of the *document* you're working on, which can be much larger than the screen itself. You view documents through *windows*. *Disk drives* "read" the information stored on magnetic *floppy disks*.

You have your choice about how you want your computer configured, or set up: an SE might come with two internal floppy disk drives, or it may have one floppy drive and one internal *hard disk*, which is like a huge floppy disk encased inside the body of the computer. You can also purchase external *peripheral* hard disks that sit underneath or next to your computer. The CPU (the central, or *computer processing unit*) itself processes (but cannot store) information; the disks are used to store, or *save,* that information.

HARDWARE CATEGORIES

There are five basic functional categories of hardware that go into a computer configuration, or setup:

- Personal computers
- Monitors
- Input devices
- Storage devices
- Output devices

Everyone who uses a computer probably also uses all of these other kinds of hardware, as they are integral to the function of the computer unit itself.

Above, a Macintosh II computer, shown here with an Apple 13" RGB color monitor, an extended keyboard, and a mouse.

Personal computers

All Macintosh CPUs are what is known as personal computers, or small processing units designed primarily for use by individuals. Macintosh computers run on system software unique to the Macintosh, known as the Macintosh Operating System, or OS. Some other common computer operating systems are the DOS system, which runs a number of personal computers such as IBM and Compac, and

the UNIX operating system, which runs Sun workstations.

There are now several models of Macintosh computers available on the market: two smaller, self-contained CPUs, the Mac Plus and the Mac SE; three larger, multi-unit CPUs, the Mac II, IIcx, and IIci; and the portable laptop Mac.

Monitors

Both the Plus and the SE have built-in black and white monitors, but although you can only view work in black and white, you can work on color files—as long as you're able to visualize what you're working on! The Mac II series allows you to both work and view in full color. Their color screen displays are made up of a combination of red, green, and blue (RGB) which, when combined onscreen, give the effect of a full range of colors. RGB monitors allow you to view facsimiles of PMS (Pantone Matching System) colors and process colors (magenta, cyan,

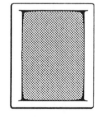

Left, a full-page black and white peripheral monitor manufactured by a third party developer, which connects to the main computer unit via cabling.

yellow, and black)—the two color standards of the graphics industry. Screens on these larger CPUs are not built-in, giving you the option to purchase either the standard

Apple 13" RGB monitor, or pick from one of the many monitors made by other manufacturers (known in the industry as "third-party developers").

Input devices

All Macintosh CPUs come with a basic Macintosh keyboard and mouse (shown, left, with the Macintosh II), the two primary means of entering data into the processing unit. The typewriter-like keyboard allows you to type data (words and numbers) and commands; the mouse allows you to enter selections and actions by pointing to, and using, icons, tools, and commands onscreen.

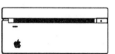

A disk drive that "reads" a 3.5" floppy disk when it is inserted into the "port" in the face of the drive.

Disk drives, which "read" data off of storage disks, and modems, which allow data to be transmitted to the computer via the phone lines, can also be considered input devices.

Another kind of input device is scanners, which are used to enter flat images like drawn sketches, continuous-tone photographs, and even manuscripts into the CPU. Art and sketches can be scanned and saved as line-art (high-contrast,

Process, view, input, store, and output— the five functional tasks covered by hardware

Apple is not the only manufacturer of hardware for use with the Macintosh line of computers. Other companies, known as "third-party developers" manufacture and sell hardware such as scanners, modems, hard disks, keyboards, and printers.
A good way to comparison shop hardware is to read the comparitive reviews in the Macintosh magazines, such as *Macworld, Publish, MacWeek,* and *MacUser.*

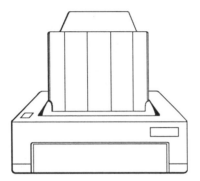

A scanner, which is an input device used to "read" flat images such as sketches and photographs, and to enter them into the computer processing unit

non-digitized), for use as "for position only" art in layouts and mechanicals, or as MacPaint files (digitized, or pixelated, images), to be used as templates to trace over in one of the more sophisticated drawing programs like Adobe Illustrator. Photographs can be digitized and used in mechanicals. They can also be manipulated and edited in "image manipulation" programs like ImageStudio and Digital Darkroom. Optical Character Recognition (OCR) devices can "read" manuscripts—which saves you from having to retype material that's already been typed or typeset. OCR software varies in accuracy and can misread characters, so it must always be closely proofed.

Video digitizers are another kind of input device, which, like video cameras, allow you to shoot three-dimensional images, and digitize them so that they can be entered into the CPU.

Storage devices

The computer itself processes data but it cannot store it. There are several kinds of storage devices commonly used to store the work created on computers. The most common form of storage is on a disk. Disks are electronic storage media, not unlike cassette tapes or CDs. The most common are the small, portable 3.5" floppy disk and the larger hard disks, which may be built into the computer, or can be separate, external peripherals.

Output devices

Documents that you create on the computer can be printed out on any one of several kinds of output devices, or printers. Some are small, low-cost, low-to medium-quality printers suitable for personal use, such as the ImageWriter and LaserWriter. These are considered "proof quality" printers. For camera-ready artwork, a larger, more expensive, profe-

sional quality high-resolution typesetting machine must be used. These can be quite expensive, and are usually available

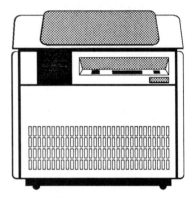

A professional Linotronic typesetting machine

at typesetters or at service bureaus, companies that specialize in providing Macintosh output to the public on a per-page basis. You can output onto regular copier paper, for proofing; onto repro typesetting paper, for pasteups; or onto negative or positive film, for sending straight to the printer. Many illustration and some page layout programs allow you to separate mechanical PMS colors and/or process colors into true color separations, output the seps onto negative film, proof them by making a conventional matchprint proof, and send the film negs and color proofs straight to the printer for stripping.

A proof-quality LaserWriter printer

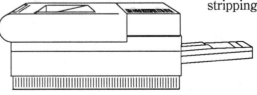

PERSONAL COMPUTERS

The Macintosh Plus

This was one of the first Macintoshes, and it is still widely in use as an entry-level computer. It's the least expensive of the Macintoshes, and is shown here sitting on an Apple hard disk, with a standard keyboard and mouse in front. The keyboard and mouse are called input devices because they are the means by which you enter information into your computer. The hard disk is a storage device—it holds your programs and type fonts. The Plus is a black and white processing unit with a 9" diagonal built-in B&W screen, but it can allow you to use (but not to view) many color programs, with the exception of pixelated color illustration programs. In fact, the Plus can do most of the same tasks an SE or II can do; it just runs slower.

The Macintosh Plus

The Macintosh SE

The newer, more expensive Macintosh SE model looks and acts a lot like the Mac Plus. Outside, it has characteristic indented stripes across its front, a smaller, more refined mouse and a more elegant keyboard design. Inside, it differs from the Plus by having what is called an "open architecture," which means it can be opened up and customized by its owner to give it increased speed, memory, and other features unavailable to Plus owners. The SE can be purchased in several different configurations, including the choice of either two internal 800k floppy disk drives, or only one internal floppy disk drive and a built-in hard disk in your choice of several different sizes. Some users who like the convenience of two internal floppy ports, but still want the mass storage of a hard disk, purchase an external hard disk from a third-party developer and set it underneath or alongside their CPU. Like the Plus, the SE can run many color programs, but, because it has only the black and white built-in screen, you can only view that work in black and white. Large-screen B&W monitors, like the one shown here behind the SE, can be purchased and connected to the SE with cabling, if desired.

The Macintosh SE with a full-page monitor (behind)

The Mac II series

These are currently the top-end products in the Macintosh family. At first glance these machines look more like the IBM PC than a Macintosh, because the processing unit and screen are separate pieces. However the user interface and operating system are definitely Macintosh. Shown here with the extended keyboard, the Mac II offers increased processing speed and a 13" Apple RGB color monitor. The IIx, IIcx and IIci look much like the II, except they have a somewhat smaller sized main processing unit (no reflection on processing capability, just a more efficient design). These machines are aimed at high-powered technical users, such as artists, engineers, designers, illustrators, or others who need extra processing speed or the ability to view graphics on a color monitor. Although there are a few special programs that will only run on the II series, most software will run on all Macintosh computers, and work the same way. Most files can be opened, and worked on, on any of these machines interchangeably.

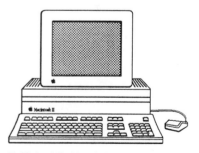

The Macintosh II with an Apple color monitor

INPUT DEVICES

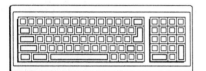

The Macintosh keyboard

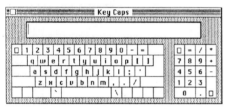

The Key Caps dialog box

The Command, Apple, or Control key

The mouse

The Keyboard

The keyboard is one of several means by which information can be input, or entered into a computer, and is still the primary means of input in some non-Macintosh operating systems. Data (words and numbers) and programming commands are typed in on the typewriter-like keyboard at left, or on the numeric keypad on its right. The cabling connecting the keyboard plugs into a special port in the back of the CPU.

Key Caps This is a handy desk accessory that allows you to open a dialog box (shown at left) that shows the exact position on your keyboard for any special symbol or character, such as © or ®, or foreign language accent available in any font family you choose to use. Holding down the caps, shift, or option keys separately or in combination will display other character sets in the Key Caps dialog box.

Special keys In addition to the standard letter and number keys found on the typical typewriter keyboard, the computer keyboard has additional keys that perform special functions. There is a Delete, or backspace key, that backspaces over previously typed characters and erases them. There is a Caps Lock key that, when depressed, causes all subsequent copy typed to appear in all caps. The Command key, when depressed while another key or combination of keys is depressed, causes a command to take effect. It is identified by the Apple logo and a pretzel-like symbol on its face, and is located near the lower left-hand side of the keyboard. There are four arrow keys that, when pressed, move the blinking insertion bar, or insertion point, in the direction of the arrow. Both the Enter key and the Return key can be used as keyboard shortcuts for selecting highlighted (default) buttons in dialog boxes, for example, the OK button. The Return key also makes the insertion point jump to the beginning of the next line, and creates "hard returns" (indicators of new paragraphs) in word-processing programs. The Shift key causes letters to be typed in caps or, when two symbols appear on the face of a key, causes the uppermost symbol to be typed. Similarly, the Option key allows you to type special symbols, such as © or ®, or foreign symbols and accent marks. The Tab key allows you to jump the insertion bar to preset tab markers. It is also a shortcut used to jump from "field" (box) to field in dialog boxes and, for example, spreadsheet programs.

The mouse

The mouse is a Xerox Company invention that has revolutionized user interface. It's essentially a remote control device that enables the user to simply point to an object or a command on the screen, and to activate that selection by pressing a button on the top of the mouse. Correct position of the mouse is shown at left: the "tail" faces away from the user, with the button in position for the index finger. Combined with the unique Macintosh interface system of windows, icons, and pull-down menus, it provides an intuitive, user-friendly means of communicating with the computer. Because a novice can quickly learn to point to pictographic icons and English-language commands in the menus, the time spent learning complex keyboard commands or a programming language is eliminated, and training time is decreased.

Floppy disk drives

The mechanisms that "read" information from, and "write" information to disks are called disk drives. In a large hard disk, both the reading mechanism and the disk itself are permanently encased together inside a hard plastic shell. The smaller, portable floppy disks must be inserted into a separate disk drive in order to be read to or from. All Macintoshes come with at least one built-in, internal disk drive for floppy disks. The SE can be purchased with a second optional internal disk drive port if desired. You can also purchase additional peripheral floppy disk drives. Having two disk drives gives you the advantage of being able to easily copy information from one disk onto another disk, a frequently necessary task. If you have more than one disk drive, it doesn't matter which disk you insert into which port.

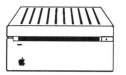

An external peripheral floppy disk drive

Scanners

Entering two-dimensional visual information into the computer requires reading the image with a piece of hardware called a scanner. Scanners interpret visual data as either line art or as digitized art. Flat art is either placed on a glass platen (like a copier machine) or run through on a drum or roller where it is read. Special software that comes with the scanner, and that you install on your computer, allows you to select preferences and options such as the size of the image area to be scanned, the type of composition desired: line art, halftone or grayscale, the resolution, or number of dots per inch, and others. Once the scanner has read the visual image, it records it in digital form based on the instructions you gave it. Scanned images can be used as templates in drawing programs, as "for position only" artwork in page layouts, and as actual line art or photographs. Scanned halftone and grayscale images can be manipulated, edited, changed, or corrected later using special image manipulation software programs such as ImageStudio, ColorStudio, PhotoShop, and Digital Darkroom. With special Optical Character Recognition (OCR) software such as OmniPage you can even scan most typewritten, and some typeset, copy in order to avoid rekeyboarding (retyping).

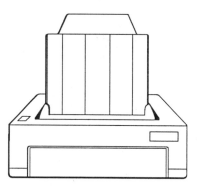

One of several kinds of scanners

Video digitizers

Entering three-dimensional visual data requires shooting the image with a video digitizer, essentially a video camera that reads three-dimensional images, converts them to two dimensions, records them in digital form using specialized software, and saves them to a disk. As with a regular scanner, the user operates the software and selects preferences through the computer processing unit, which drives the input device.

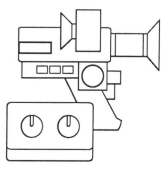

A video digitizer camera

Graphics tablets

The graphics tablet, yet another device used to input visual data into the computer, is a combination of a flat, pressure-sensitive surface, the tablet, which is keyed to a matrix of points onscreen, and a stylus, or pen, with which images are "drawn" onto the surface of the tablet. Like a mouse, the images that are traced onto the tablet correspond to the screen image—like drawing a picture onto one piece of paper and having it show up on another. However, many illustrators, once they are accustomed to drawing with the mouse, find the use of the graphics tablet superfluous.

MONITORS

A Mac SE showing its built-in, 9" diagonal B&W monitor

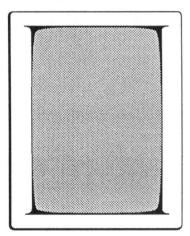

A full-page peripheral monitor

Built-in monitors

Both the Mac Plus and the SE come with built-in black and white 9" diagonal monitors. The small size of the monitors does not limit the size of the work that can be done on these computers, however; even large documents can be created, and can be moved around inside the viewing area of the screen so that all parts of the work can be seen—just not all at once. In order to overcome this inability to see the entire document at one time, most software programs have a choice of "viewing modes," which allow the user to zoom in on, or away from, an image. Closeup views let you see the details in an illustration or a line of type; far away views allow you to see the overall layout, or composition.

Black and white peripheral monitors

There are several manufacturers of excellent full- and two-page black and white monitors on the market, which are particularly useful for page layout, design, and illustration (except where color viewing is important). These monitors can be used with the SE and, in a few cases, with the Plus.

Color and grayscale monitors

These monitors offer the full range of viewing capabilities: in addition to black and white images, they show facsimiles of PMS (Pantone Matching System) colors and process (magenta, cyan, yellow, and black) colors using a combination of red, green, and blue (RGB) screen colors. They also display photographs in grayscale, which approximates the effect of continuous tone. The resolution, brightness, contrast, and other factors involved in the apparent visual quality of these monitors varies from brand to brand, and the type of work that will be viewed on them should be taken into consideration when purchasing one.

WYSIWYG, Display PostScript, and beyond

The screen resolution of all monitors is much coarser than the actual work that can be created on the Macintosh in most software programs, but although this discrepancy between what you see and what you get is jarring at first, it is a tremendous improvement over most monitors of the not-so-distant past, on which no visual representation of your work was possible. The ability of the Macintosh to create a screen representation of a file, based on programming codes, is referred to as WYSIWYG (pronounced wizzy-wig), or What You See Is What You Get. Already today's sophisticated user is clamoring for finer screen resolution, and answers to the display problem do exist. Adobe Systems has developed a screen display called Display PostScript, which is very sharp and clear—but also very new and expensive. Already available in Steve Jobs' new line of NeXT computers, it may be a few years before it becomes a standard in the Macintosh world. Other solutions to the screen display quality problem are being developed, however, including a clever solution from Letraset in their headline type manipulation program, LetraStudio, which makes use of the current capabilities of the color monitor to visually smooth the "jaggies" (the rough edges of pixels) so noticeable onscreen in large-scale type display.

STORAGE DEVICES

Floppy disks

Disks are electronic storage devices like cassette tapes except that they are very fragile, thin (hence "floppy"), and round, like records or CDs. They are stored inside thin plastic cases to protect them. Disk drives "read" information off the disks with heads, like a record player. The head itself moves, and the disk spins in its case, looking up data stored in different places on the disk. Every time you save data to a disk, it is stored at a specific "address" where it can later be found. When you initialize a disk (see below), you "partition" it, or, in effect, lay down a map of cities, streets, and mailbox addresses. The data you save "moves into" a specific address where the computer will know where to look for it the next time you want to use it.

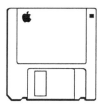

A 3.5" floppy disk case; the disk itself is permanently encased inside this small plastic container

The 3.5" double-sided, double-density (DSDD) floppy disk is the "cassette tape" of the Macintosh. It holds 800k of storage—enough for dozens of documents. Early Macintoshes (such as the old 512 model) used single-sided disks with only 400k of storage. That's why today, when you purchase or initialize a new disk, you can choose whether you want 400k or 800k.

Initializing a disk When you first put a new, blank disk into the disk drive, your Mac will ask you whether you want to initialize the disk as "single" or "double-sided." If you're using a model 512 or 512K Macintosh, select single; if you're using a Plus, an SE, a Mac II or IIcx, select double-sided. A dialog box will appear asking you what you want to name the disk; type in the name on the keyboard. If you change your mind, you can always rename the disk later when it's on the Desktop. If you want to erase a used disk so that you can reuse it, insert the disk into the disk drive, select the disk icon when it appears on the Desktop, and then select the command Erase Disk from the Special menu on the Desktop. **CAUTION:** Do not erase or initialize a disk unless you are sure that there are no valuable files or applications on that disk. **NEVER** erase your hard disk.

Internal and external hard disks

Several makes of large-capacity internal (meaning that it's built into your computer) and external (peripheral, or not built in) hard disks are available. Except for the fact that one is built in and the other is not, they're exactly the same thing. Shown at right is the Apple 20MB SCSI (pronounced "scuzzy") external hard disk. Other fine quality hard disks are made by third-party developers.

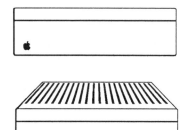

Front and top/front view of an Apple SCSI external hard disk drive

An external hard disk is like a giant floppy disk, enclosed with the head that reads the disk inside a plastic box. Connected to your computer unit via cabling, it allows you to install all your applications and type fonts directly onto the hard disk, where they are always available for your immediate use without having to insert a floppy disk. This frees up your floppy disk drives to use for saving your own document files onto floppy disks, a commonly recommended system of disk and file management. Hard Disks are large storage devices; they usually start at about 20MB in size, the equivalent of literally thousands of floppy disks.

OUTPUT DEVICES

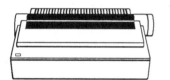

A 72 dpi ImageWriter printer

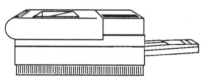

A 300 dpi Apple LaserWriter printer

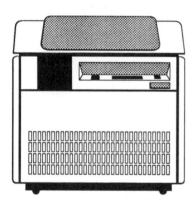

A 1270 dpi Linotronic 100 typesetting machine

The ImageWriter

The ImageWriter is the lowest end of the output devices in both cost and quality. It is a dot matrix printer the produces bit-mapped (not PostScript) output at a resolution of 72 dots-per-inch (dpi) on hand-fed 8-1/2" sheets of paper or on continuous pin-fed fan-fold computer paper.

The LaserWriter

Apple LaserWriters are PostScript printers: output devices of affordable cost and medium quality—good enough for proofing and for comps, but not for professional-quality final output. They can produce output at a resolution of 300 dpi on cassette-fed copier paper, in letter or legal size. Each comes with a number of "resident" (or pre-installed) type fonts, such as Helvetica and Times Roman and, more importantly, can print downloadable PostScript typefaces accurately. Downloadable type fonts are fonts produced and sold by third-party developers; you purchase and install them into your System, and the computer "downloads" them, meaning that it sends the Post-Script files describing the fonts to your printer when you send a document to print.

Linotronic and Compugraphic typesetting machines

These are top-quality typesetting machines that produce the highest quality resolution output. Their very high cost makes them impractical for use except through commercial typesetting companies, or service bureaus. They produce output on phototypesetting paper or film at a resolution of from 1270 dpi, on the Linotronic 100, to 2540 dpi, on the Linotronic 300. These machines are most commonly used for output of repro-quality typeset pages created in page layout programs, and for output of negative film color separations from illustration or page layout programs.

QMS and Tektronic printers

These are medium resolution (300 dpi) full-color output devices, suitable for rough color comps, color checks, or samples. Their coarse resolution makes them less than satisfactory for use in viewing or comping colored type, because at 300 dpi the dots in the type tend to break up letterforms. But they are extremely useful for proofing illustrations, especially when made primarily of large blocks of solid color. They can save the expense of seeing an illustration for the first time at the chromalin proof stage, which cannot occur until after expensive color separations have been made.

Other brands of printers

There are many other brands of printers and typesetting machines, aimed variously at users who demand low-cost, high-speed, special paper loading or collating capabilities, maximum type font capability, or other features. The resolution of these printers varies: for example, the Compugraphic 400-PS prints out at 400 dpi, and the Varityper VT-600 prints at 600 dpi.

Chapter 4: The Desktop

The *Desktop* is "home base" for the Macintosh. It is the place that you enter when you turn the computer on, and the place that you exit from when you turn the computer off. It is the place from which you enter into *application* programs, and where you return to when you exit an application. The Desktop, with its combination of pictorial *icons*, pull-down *menus,* and *windows,* is famous for the easy-to-learn Macintosh *user interface.* The *Finder* is the invisible, or background, application that runs the Desktop and performs all the functions that you do there, like opening and closing *files* and *folders*, and naming, moving, viewing, duplicating, and saving them.

Illustration by Max Seabaugh and Laura Lamar in SuperPaint, with images from Hypercard.

THE DESKTOP: WINDOWS, MENUS, & ICONS

The Desktop is "home base" on the Macintosh: you enter into all applications from it, and return to it when you exit an application.

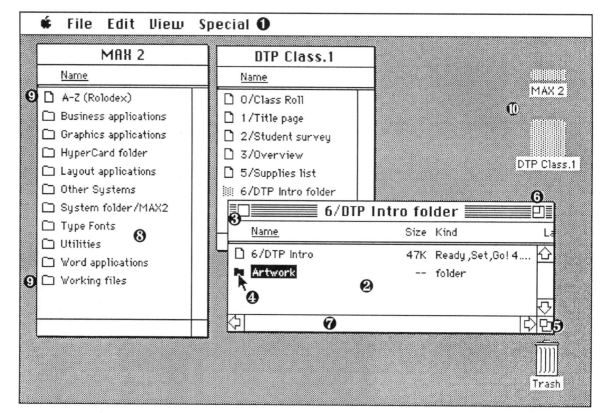

1 The menu bar appears across the top of the Desktop (as well as every application); you "pull down" menus of commands from it.

2 The currently active window, which always has gray stripes across the top; open, close, and zoom boxes; and scroll bars and arrows.

3 The close box. Click once inside this box with the tip of the selection arrow (pointer) to close the currently active window.

4 The pointer and a selected (highlighted) folder. Click once with the tip of the arrow on the folder icon to select it, twice to open it.

5 The size box: drag on it to resize the window.

6 The zoom box: click on it to jump from current window size, to full size, and back again.

7 The horizontal scroll bar, with scrolling arrows at both ends: click on the scroll arrows to move the viewing area of the screen in the direction you want to make visible. If there is more data in the window than can be seen at its current size, a scroll box will appear inside a gray scroll bar.

8 Directory listings. These are the names of the documents and folders inside the folder or disk that the directory window represents. Double-click on any disk or folder icon to see a directory listing of its contents.

9 A folder icon looks like a manila file folder. At the top of this list is a document icon, which looks like a small page with the corner turned down.

10 The hard disk icon, top, and a floppy disk icon, below. When gray, it means that they are "open" and that their directory listings are visible in an open window on the Desktop, as shown above.

SETTING UP & MANAGING THE DESKTOP

The hierarchical filing system (HFS)

The Macintosh Desktop makes use of a filing system not unlike the one you probably already use in the desk drawers and filing cabinets in your home or office.

The desktop metaphor

The documents you create and save using software applications are called files—regardless of whether they are illustrations, letters, or databases. Files can sit out on top of your desk, where you can move them, stack them one on top of another, put them in drawers or in folders, or throw them in the trash. When your desk gets messy, you clean it up by filing things or throwing them away.

Creating folders

The hierarchical filing system allows you to create empty file folders, name them, nest folders within folders and put them wherever you want. You use these folders to store your files in. To create an empty file on your Desktop, just hold down the Command key and type N. A new, untitled folder will appear. Select the type below the folder with the I-beam tool (which appears when you pass the selection arrow over the type). When the type is highlighted, you can type in a new name for that folder.

Organizing files

Everyone has their own favorite system for setting up their filing system; here are a few ideas:

The file cabinet

If you have a hard disk, you can use it as you would a large filing cabinet filled with folders. If you only use a few programs, a simple approach would be to store all your software applications in one folder, and all your working files in another. If you have too many files in a folder, however, it will become difficult to find what you're looking for when you open up a folder. Nesting folders within folders allows you to create a hierarchy of storage, hiding files several layers deep within folders and keeping it easy to find things.

Filing by kind

Another approach, and one better suited to the computer user with lots of software and document files, is to create a folder for each kind of software application, such as shown in the hard disk directory on the page opposite. Accounting, database, and management programs are kept together in one folder labeled Business; drawing, painting, illustration, and image manipulation applications are kept together in a folder labeled Graphics; a choice of several popular page layout programs are kept in yet another folder labeled Layout. Since all the applications stored on your hard disk are copies of your

purchased originals, you can store your valuable original application disks in a safe place.

Working files

The user of the Desktop shown at left keeps all her working files on floppy disks, but stores a few current files on the Desktop in a folder labeled Working Files. There are several good reasons to store working files on floppies:

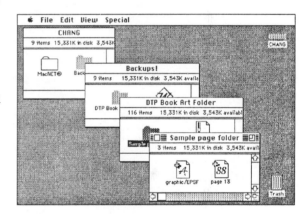

they are easily transportable, they are kept in manageably small units for easy backup, and, in the event of a disaster such as a power outage or hard disk failure, only the file currently in use risks being lost. Although it rarely happens, if ever you lose the entire contents of your hard disk, you'll be glad that you didn't store all your original files in one place.

A folder within a folder within a folder... Shown above are the open directory windows for three nested folders. Note how each opened folder icon is grayed back, and how the name of each folder appears at the top of its opened directory.

Viewing

The Desktop gives you a choice of how to view your files inside your folders. It is a matter of personal preference whether you choose to view your Desktop by name, by icon, or by another of the several viewing choices available to you under the View menu.

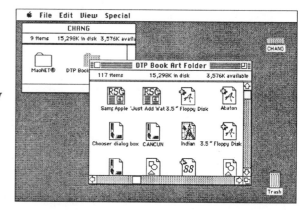

directory window, the window will appear as a scrolling window (below left), letting you know that there are files hidden at the end of the directory list.

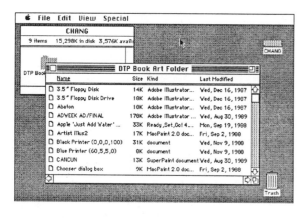

The directory window above shows files viewed by name, with the file size, kind of application, and day, date, and time of last save listed after the document name.

Viewing by name, etc. Viewing by name, date, size or kind ensures that all the contents of a disk or folder will be arranged in list form from the top of the directory window down, arranged either alphabetically, by document name; by date (of the last time the document was saved); by size (how many kilobytes large the file is); or by kind (all the MacWrite files together, all the MacPaint files together). Each listed item tells the document name, file size, application used to create the file, and date and time of last save. If there are more files than can be viewed all at once in the

View by icon When you choose to view by icon or by small icon, all the files will be represented by pictorial icons spread out across the directory window. Each file will be represented by a specific icon that tells you what software application that file was originally created in, with the name of the specific file centered underneath that icon. Sometimes when names are too long they overlap and obscure one another. Rearranging the icons may be necessary in order to read all the names clearly. View by Icon does not tell you the size of the file or the date or time of the last save.

However, in a few instances, viewing by icon does provide additional, important information that you can't see under View by Name. For example, when you create and save an Adobe Illustrator file, its icon is a simple Illustrator program

icon. But once that file has been changed to an Encapsulated Post-Script (EPS) file for importation into a page layout program, a bold plus mark is added to the upper left-hand corner of the Illustrator icon (above). If you're ever not sure whether you saved an illustration as an EPS file or not, viewing by icon will tell you.

Another time viewing by icon can give you extra information is when you're switching from one startup system to another. When a System folder is activated, its icon appears with a small Macintosh icon inside the folder icon. When a System folder has been deactivated, the folder icon is empty.

The directory window above shows documents viewed by icon. Here the icons have been moved so that all the names are visible and don't overlap one another. The icons can also be staggered to accommodate long names.

** ✦ File   Edit   View   Special**

The Apple menu

The very first pull-down menu on the menu bar of the Desktop—as well as within every application—is indicated by the Apple logo and is called the Apple menu. Under the Apple menu you can find mini-applications known as *desk accessories*. You can customize your selection of desk accessories to suit your tastes, but basic desk accessories that come with your computer allow you to select a printer, set preference settings, find lost files, and look up information about whatever program is currently running.

About... is the first selection available under the Apple menu, and it tells you the name of the application that is currently running. For example, if you're at the Desktop, it will say About the Finder. When you select it, a dialog box (frequently the startup screen of the application) will appear, telling you the version number of that particular application, the amount of memory it takes up, and other pertinent information.

Control Panel This desk accessory allows you to select user preferences for everything from the speed of your mouse and blinking insertion bar, to the loudness of your beep sound. You can create new Desktop

background patterns by clicking in the checkerboard box to add and delete pixels, then click on the little Desktop icon to its

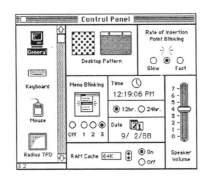

right to activate the new pattern. You can change the date and time of the clock; important to remember when the time changes occur, as this clock sets the recorded date and time of your last save when you work on files.

Find file is an accessory that comes with the Macintosh and that enables you to search for files throughout your hierarchical filing system, by typing in the name—or a portion of the name—of the file that you're looking for. When it's found, a diagram mapping a route through the folder hierarchy will tell you where you can find your file.

The File menu

The File menu is always the second pull-down menu on the Desktop and in your software applications, and it always has a similar selection of commands. The File menu is always the place to open (Command-O) or close (Command-W) an existing file, create a new file or folder (Command-N), print a file (Command-P), or quit an application (Command-Q). You can also find out about any file or application by selecting its name or icon with the pointer and typing Command-I, which will bring up a dialog box telling you the version number of the application, the amount of memory it takes up, and other pertinent information. You can also duplicate any selected file by choosing Duplicate (Command-D) from the File menu. It will call the copy "Copy of..." until you rename the new file.

The Edit Menu

The Edit menu is always the third pull-down menu, and lets you cut (Command-X), copy (Command-C), and paste (Command-V) any selected item. When you cut or copy an item, it is temporarily pasted into the Clipboard, where it is stored until it's replaced by cutting or pasting something else. To view the current contents of the Clipboard while on the Desktop, select that command from the Edit menu.

One of the most useful commands you can know is available under the Edit menu: Command-Z, or Undo. It lets you bail out of a mistake before it's too late, and it works in almost every application. In fact, some programs have up to 99 levels of undo! Whenever you make a mistake, just type Command-Z, and it will undo the last move you made. Be sure to do it immediately, though, as it only undoes *the last move made.*

TO TURN OFF THE MAC

It's easy to turn your Mac on, but use this safe procedure for turning it off or the information on your disks could be damaged or lost.

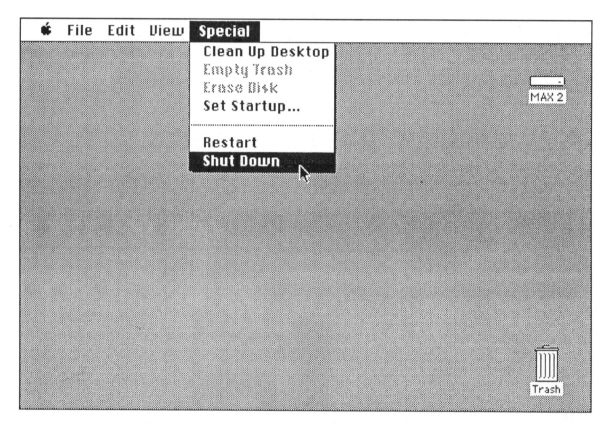

1 Save: If you are still in an application, save your work by choosing Save (Command-S) from the File menu. Exit the application by choosing Quit (Command-Q) from the File menu.

2 Close: Close (Command-W) all open windows on the screen, including the hard disk directory, so that your Desktop looks like the one pictured above. **TIP:** A shortcut that closes *all* open windows quickly is to hold down the Option key while clicking once in the close box of the active window. All open windows will zoom shut.

3 Click: Click anywhere on the Desktop to de-select the hard and floppy disk icons. They should be white, not black, like the hard disk icon shown above. This prevents them from being accidently erased when you pull down the Special menu.

4 Shut Down: Select Shut Down from the Special menu (as shown above). A dialog box will appear telling you that it's okay to shut down (to be sure not to erase your disks accidentally, see step 3 above).

5 Turn Off: Turn off the power switch (on the SE, it's at the back of the Macintosh on the lower left side; Mac IIs turn off at the keyboard).

The illustration above is called a screen dump or screen capture. It is created using the Camera desk accessory (or typing Command-Shift-3), which saves the file as a MacPaint document.

Chapter 5: Software

Software is the generic name for the application programs that we run on the computer to perform specific tasks. Different categories of software are "specialists" in different kinds of tasks, such as word processing programs for writing and editing text, graphics programs for creating graphics or illustrations, page layout programs for setting type and creating electronic page layouts, spreadsheet programs for performing accounting or spreadsheet functions, and database programs for keeping files of information like rolodexes and billing records. Word processing, graphics and page layout programs are the three kinds most often used by graphic designers.

Illustration by Laura Lamar in Adobe Illustrator and Ready,Set,Go!

ABOUT SOFTWARE TYPES & SELECTION

Text is written, edited, and proofed in a word processing program . . .

Illustrations and charts are drawn in graphics programs . . .

. . . and both are imported into page layout programs, where the text is type speced, the illustrations sized, and both placed in a page layout.

Choosing software

Software programs, or applications, are electronic files that you purchase to help you accomplish specific tasks on the Macintosh. Each software package is designed to accomplish a certain set of tasks in very specific ways. Choosing the right software package for the right job is very important.

Categories Software is available in many broad categories: word processing, graphics, page layout, scanning and image editing, accounting and spreadsheet, database, presentation, and others. Some software manufacturers offer whole families of related software; others may market a single specialized product. All software products for the Macintosh can be used to create parts of a job, each according to its abilities, and then the separate parts are brought together in one format, such as a layout program.

Read the reviews Before you purchase software, you should first read up on all the current products available. There are many good Macintosh publications on the market that publish product reviews and comparisons: you might check *Publish, Macworld, MacWeek,* or *MacUser* magazines for the latest contenders.

Needs and compatibility Keep in mind your own specific needs, and if you can, also visit Mac-using friends and ask them what their favorite programs are, and why. If you work with a group of people you may want to purchase the same set of programs in order to be compatible; when everyone in a work group uses the same programs, you can open and exchange each others' files.

Representative types

Because there are so many software programs available today, we have selected a few programs to cover in this book that are either easy-to-learn basics, are in widespread use, are classic examples of their type, or are just plain good.

Word processing For this category, we chose MacWrite, still one of the simplest, best, and most widely available word processing programs. Once you've learned MacWrite, you'll know the fundamental tasks common to all word processing applications, and it should be easy to learn Microsoft Word or another advanced program later—if you so desire.

Bit-mapped graphics or paint programs The first Macintosh graphics programs were all bit-mapped, or pixelated, programs. Today's bit-mapped programs have come a long way, and even include highly sophisticated full-color painting programs. Our introductory choice is SuperPaint, a stalwart classic that will teach you the essentials of working with bitmaps, and prepare you for future forays into such advanced color painting programs as PixelPaint or Studio 8.

PostScript drawing programs

These programs are classics for drawing line art, technical illustrations, and graphic art. They excel at crisp, smooth lines and curves, and solid or shaded areas of color. Adobe Illustrator, our choice, will teach you how PostScript programs work and how best to make use of their capabilities. Later, you may wish to explore Aldus FreeHand, another drawing program that can also manipulate type extensively, or to design type fonts in Fontographer, a program that lets you create type fonts using tools very similar to those in Illustrator.

Page layout programs There are three top page layout programs for the Mac available on the market: PageMaker, the earliest program available, is still the most widely used because of its reliability and ease of use. Two superior but lesser-known programs, Quark XPress and Ready,Set,Go!, offer a high degree of control and advanced typographic capabilities. Ready,Set,Go!, our choice, combines the ease-of-use and freedom of movement of PageMaker with the precise control of XPress.

ANATOMY OF A DISK

This is a 3.5" floppy disk for the Macintosh.

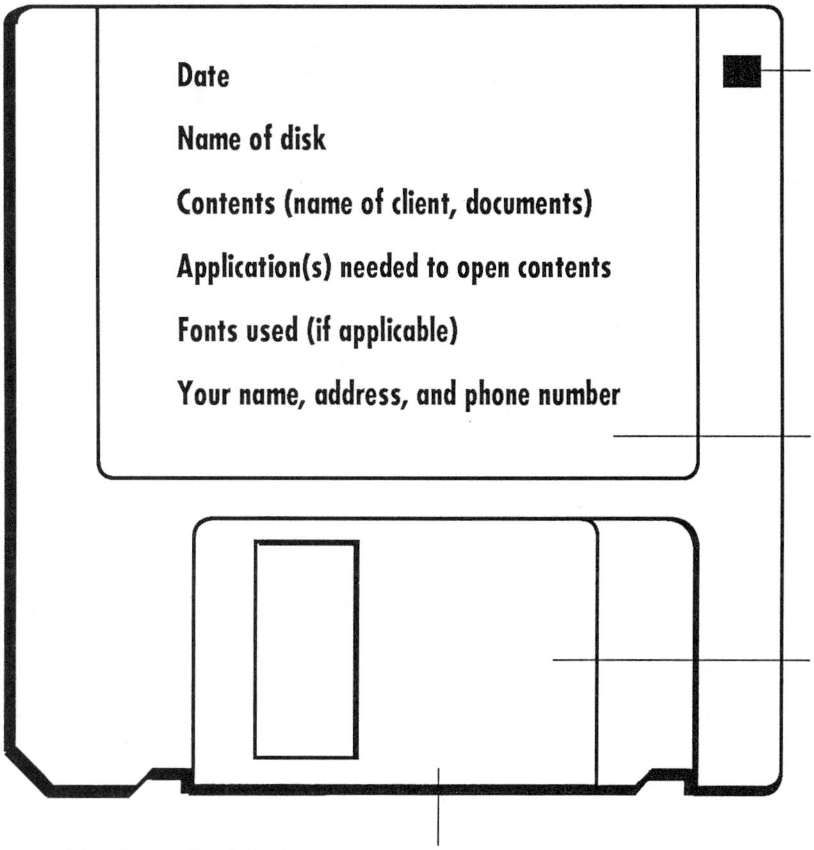

Date

Name of disk

Contents (name of client, documents)

Application(s) needed to open contents

Fonts used (if applicable)

Your name, address, and phone number

Disk locking mechanism (on back) Slide button up to lock disk, down to unlock. From the front of the disk, if you can see through this hole, the disk is locked; if it is filled with black, it is unlocked. You can open and read a locked disk, but cannot save to it until it is unlocked.

Disk label Attach to front of disk. Include information on the disk label that will identify when it was created, what the name of the disk is, its contents, the application(s) used to create—and needed to open— the documents on it, and your name, address, and phone number.

Protective shutter When you insert the disk into the disk drive port, this shutter slides back so that the drive can "read" the magnetic disk inside. You can slide this shutter back to look at the disk inside, but don't handle it.

Initializing a disk prepares it to receive information by organizing the surface of the disk into—for want of a better metaphor— towns, streets, and houses. Data "moves into" a specific street address when it is saved, and when you want to open a file later, the computer looks for it at its last known address.

Front end and top side of the disk: Insert the disk into the drive with the label facing up, and the metallic shutter towards the drive. (The circle on back should face down.)

The 3.5" floppy disk is the "cassette tape" of the Macintosh—it is a magnetic medium, or storage device, on which you store *documents, files,* and *applications.* Floppy disks are portable, and are the medium on which *software* programs come when you purchase them.

Macintosh disks come in one size (3.5"), but with two possible capacities: 400k, or single-sided disks, for use on the older Macintosh 512 models, and 800k, or double-sided disks, for use on Plus, SE, and Mac II models.

When you first insert a new, unused disk into the *disk drive,* a dialog box will appear asking you to *initialize* the disk (make it ready to receive data). **CAUTION:** Be sure to read the definition of *initialize* on page 15 before proceeding. Select either single-sided or double-sided, depending on the type of disk you have bought and the machine you'll use it on. Then name the disk, and it's ready to use. You can rename a disk at any time at the Desktop level by highlighting its name with the I-beam tool and typing in a new name.

TO ENTER AN APPLICATION

The very first step when you enter an application and create a new document is to name it and save it to a disk.

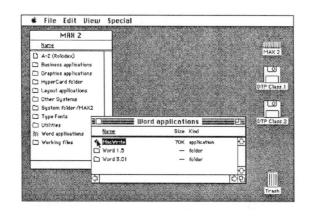

1 Open: Find the application you want to use in a folder. On this hard disk, programs are stored in folders with other applications that are similar: word processing, graphics, layout. Open the application by double-clicking on its icon (shown above, MacWrite, viewed by name).

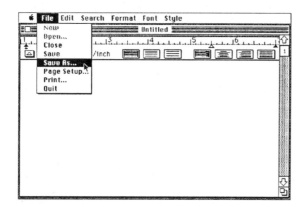

2 Save As: A window will appear labeled Untitled. Select Save As from the File menu (above).

3 Name the document: A dialog box will appear prompting you to name the document (top, right). Type a name into the box that has a blinking insertion bar (just start typing). You can correct your typing by clicking and dragging the I-beam tool over any incorrect letters and retyping them. To delete letters, just backspace over them (using the Delete key), or select them by dragging the I-beam tool over them, and then hit the Delete key.

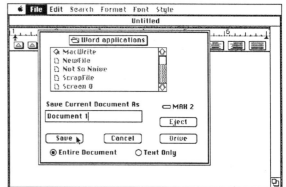

4 Save to a disk: If you want to save this document on a disk other than the current one click on the button that says Drive. You can tell which disk you're currently on by its name and icon, which usually appear just above the button labeled Eject, or near the right-hand side of the dialog box (see above). An icon—representing any other disk currently in your disk drive—will appear. You can eject a disk and insert other disks (see below) while you are here. Click Save after the icon representing the disk you want to save your document on appears. You are now ready to start work on this new document.

To eject a disk: If you want to eject the current floppy disk so that you can insert another disk, click Eject. The current disk will pop out of the disk drive, and you can insert another disk into the disk drive and save to it.

To cancel: If you change your mind or want to bail out before naming or saving, click Cancel.

5 Save changes: Remember to periodically save your work—at least every 15 minutes—while you are working. To continue to save your changes after the document has already been named, just select Save from the File menu. In some (but not all) applications, you can use the keyboard shortcut Command-S to save. **TIP:** Use Save As to save sequentially numbered versions of your work, so that you can go back to earlier versions if you want to.

TO EXIT AN APPLICATION

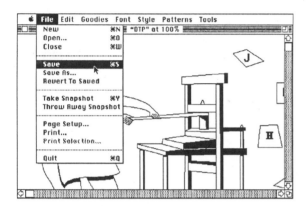

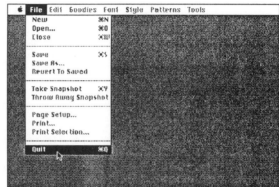

To exit an application, just remember these three steps: Save, Close, and Quit.

1 Save: When you wish to stop working on your document, first select Save from the File menu, or its keyboard shortcut, Command-S (if available in the program you're currently using, it will appear on the menu to the right of the command, as shown above).

3 Quit: The window will disappear, and you will be left with a blank gray screen. You are still in the application. In order to exit the application, select Quit from the File menu, or its keyboard shortcut Command-Q. You will return to the Desktop. **TIP:** You'll be able to tell when you're back at the Desktop because your hard disk icon (if you're using one) or floppy disk and trash can icons will appear on the right-hand side of the screen, as shown below.

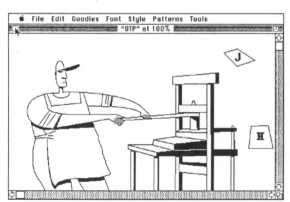

4 Move on: From the Desktop, you can now either move on, and open another document or application icon to enter another program, or you can follow the shut-down procedure (see "To Turn Off the Mac," page 36) to turn off the computer.

2 Close: Close the window by clicking on the close box in the upper left corner of the window (as shown above), by selecting Close from the File menu, or by typing its keyboard shortcut Command-W (not available—and not always the same keyboard shortcut—in all programs).

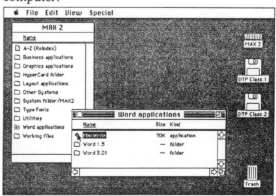

Remember, if a keyboard shortcut is available in an application, it will be listed on the pull-down menu opposite its command equivalent. If no shortcut appears on the pull-down menu, that shortcut is not available in this program.

MAC HYGIENE

The risk
Even if you don't work on a network, every time you insert a floppy disk into your Macintosh you are at risk of infection from one of the many computer viruses that are at large. Viruses have even been known to travel on purchased software disks (although rarely!) and over networks and bulletin boards.

About viruses Viruses are self-replicating strings of programming code that can travel on floppy disks, jump off floppies onto hard disks, and infect and destroy your files.

Signs of infection You won't necessarily be able to tell if or when this happens, but some possible signs that you may be infected by a virus might be frequent bombing, erractic behavior of files or applications that you've used successfully in the past, or otherwise inexplicable behavior.

What to do If you suspect a viral infection, first turn off your system. As long as your computer is on, the virus can replicate itself and jump from one application or file to another. Next, if you haven't already done so, purchase one or more good viral detection applications, such as SAM, Interferon, Virex, Virus

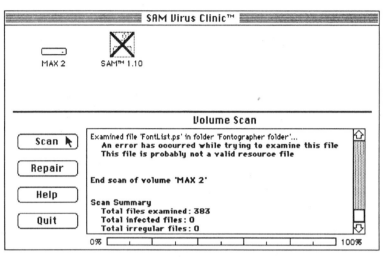

Detective, or Disinfectant, and follow the instructions to scan your hard disk and all your floppies. Some programs will identify what files are infected and even give you a printout of the infected files and the date and time of contamination, which can be useful in determining where the infection came from. You may have to discard the infected file completely, although some programs can repair infected files. To be extra safe, we always trash infected files and reinitialize infected floppies.

Keeping up-to-date Because there are so many strains of viruses, and because new ones crop up at such an alarming rate, it's crucial to stay on top of the current virus news. One of the best sources for updates is *MacWeek* magazine, which reports weekly on new virus strains and which anti-virus programs can protect against

them. No one program can cover you completely, so you may wish to purchase several. We use SAM, which scans every floppy disk as you insert it into the disk drive port, and Vaccine, Ferrit, Interferon, and Virex.

Social responsibility Like a victim of any infectious disease, you have a responsibility to others with whom you've come in contact. If you're ever infected, notify anyone with whom you've exchanged files since the first recorded date of infection on your system. They, too, stand at risk of losing valuable files, and they'll appreciate being able to catch a potential problem before it grows out of control.

SAM Virus Clinic™ automatically scans every floppy disk that you insert into your disk drive port, or gives you the option to skip a scan if, for example, you've just scanned, ejected, and reinserted a disk. You can also scan directly from the application itself. The dialog box shown at left allows you to select which disk(s) to scan (click on a disk icon to deselect it, as shown by the X). When you click Scan, a list of infected files, if any, will appear in the scrolling window, and can be printed out for later reference. You can choose whether to repair an infected file, or choose to trash it later. The bar at the bottom of the dialog box tells you what percentage of the files on the disk have been scanned.

Chapter 6: Word Processing

Word processing programs are used to write, correct, and edit text files. They can cut and paste and move words or blocks of text, and format text using type specs. They can be used to write letters, format bills and invoices, make proposals, or prepare manuscripts for importing into page layout applications. MacWrite was one of the first, and is still one of the simplest and most widely used word processing programs. It is used here as an introduction to the overall category of word processing software; the basic tasks common to most other word processing applications can be learned with this simple program.

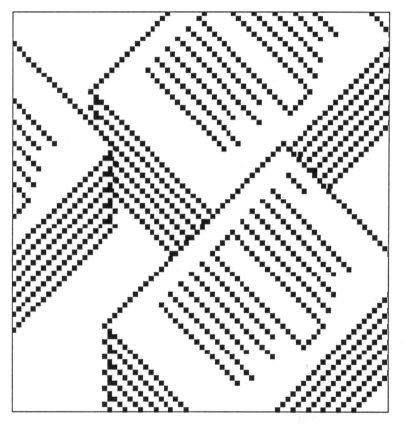

Illustration by Laura Lamar in MacPaint

ABOUT WORD PROCESSING PROGRAMS

Word processing programs are used to write, correct, and edit text files. They can be used to create files to output (print out) directly from the program, or they can be imported into

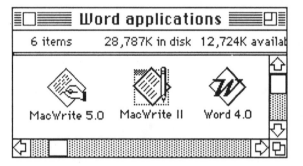

Above: The directory window of a folder containing several word processing applications, including two versions of MacWrite and the latest version of Microsoft Word. To make use of the auxiliary files that come with each program, you should store each application in a folder with its own Dictionary, Help, and other special files.

(brought into) page layout programs, where you can polish the formatting (type specifications and page design) and turn them into final page layouts.

How to choose

Today's word processing programs are so sophisticated that they overlap the capabilities of page layout programs: you can use them to spec type, set margins, tabs, and columns, and import art. Conversely, many page layout programs such as Ready,Set,Go! and Quark XPress also have built-in word processing capabilities. So how do you choose which kind of program to use?

Features Your choice of program will depend on the features needed to accomplish the task at hand. If you are preparing a page with simple type specifications, page setup, and grid structure, such as a

letter, invoice, proposal, or other business document, you may appreciate the ease of use and near-universal compatibility of a program like MacWrite. If you are preparing or receiving a manuscript, you may wish to take advantage of special features that let you count words or characters, search for "invisible" characters, search for and replace words, or check and correct spelling—features not every layout program can offer, but that most word processing programs do.

For advanced formatting and type control, including specifying fractional point sizes and leading, or kerning and letter-spacing to the hundreds or thousandths of an em, turn to a good page layout program.

Compatibility In any software program selection, you should consider compatibility with clients or others in your work group. We actually keep several word processing programs on hand simply so that we can open and edit manuscript files from the many writers, editors, and art directors that we work with. Our word processing needs are simple, and we like the ease of use, reliability, and general good behavior of MacWrite. Many professional writers we know prefer to use Microsoft Word, because of its

speed and advanced features for character counting, search and replace, invisible character display, and its ability to translate files imported from other operating systems. Be sure to check for compatibility with the page layout software you plan to use. Although most word processing programs will import into most page layout programs, some are real prima donnas and can behave less than nicely! Some programs are designed to work hand-in-hand so that style tags applied within a word processing application turn into formatted type when imported as "tagged text" into a page layout program.

Dictionaries Some of the most important files that come with your word processing program are the dictionaries, so be sure to include any dictionary files in the folder that you keep your application in. English language spelling and hyphenation dictionaries can be added to by the user, to include special client, product, or industry names and terminology, and to control if and where hyphenation will be allowed.

Fonts The fonts available to you in your word processing program will be the same fonts that are installed into your System folder (printer fonts) and into the System file (screen fonts). In other words, fonts are available system-wide, and are not limited to specific applications. For more about fonts, see Chapter 9, starting on page 81.

INTRODUCTION TO MACWRITE II

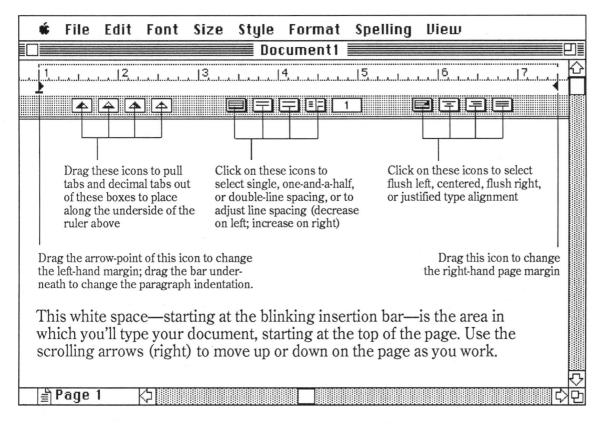

Drag these icons to pull tabs and decimal tabs out of these boxes to place along the underside of the ruler above

Click on these icons to select single, one-and-a-half, or double-line spacing, or to adjust line spacing (decrease on left; increase on right)

Click on these icons to select flush left, centered, flush right, or justified type alignment

Drag the arrow-point of this icon to change the left-hand margin; drag the bar underneath to change the paragraph indentation.

Drag this icon to change the right-hand page margin

This white space—starting at the blinking insertion bar—is the area in which you'll type your document, starting at the top of the page. Use the scrolling arrows (right) to move up or down on the page as you work.

The basic skills you'll learn in MacWrite are common to all Macintosh word processing applications.

Startup procedure

To use MacWrite, enter the application using the steps in "To Enter an Application" on page 40. When you first enter the program, there will be a blinking insertion bar in the upper left corner of the document page. You'll start typing there.

Working procedure

The beauty of word processing software is that it makes it easy to correct mistakes and move copy around, so you're free to write and not worry about typing everything perfectly the first time. You might find it helpful to first jot down subjects you want to cover and cut and paste them to make a rough outline. The outline entries can then be used as subheads under which text is written, cutting and pasting until you get the right order. It's a good idea to write first, then go back and correct mistakes and make editing decisions.

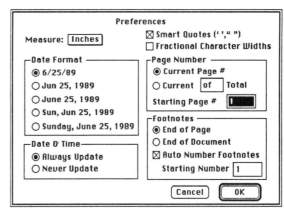

The Preferences dialog box under the Edit menu is the place to change to your preferred unit of measurement, the date format, and to select straight or curly quote defaults, as well as to set the current page number and placement of footnotes.

To correct, change, or delete copy

Select the copy you want to change by dragging the I-beam tool over that copy to highlight it. When the copy is highlighted, you can just type in the new copy, which will automatically replace the highlighted copy. Or you can press the Delete key, which will remove the highlighted copy.

A shortcut for selecting type: click twice on a word to select that word; click three times to select an entire line; click four times to select the paragraph. Many programs use some variation of this shortcut; try it and see if it works in your other applications.

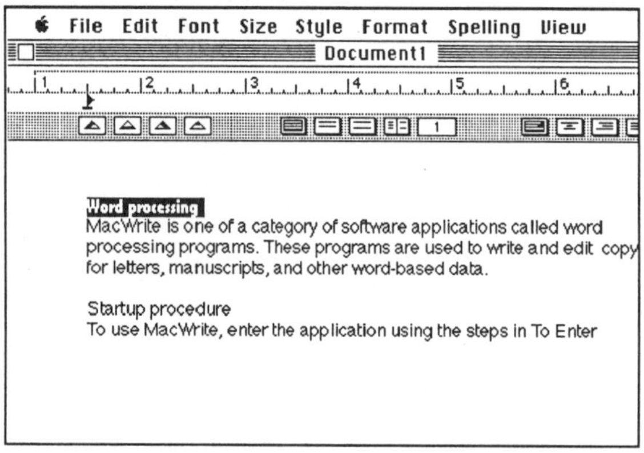

```
 File  Edit  Font  Size  Style  Format  Spelling  View
                         Document1
  |1       |2       |3       |4       |5       |6
```

Word processing
MacWrite is one of a category of software applications called word processing programs. These programs are used to write and edit copy for letters, manuscripts, and other word-based data.

Startup procedure
To use MacWrite, enter the application using the steps in To Enter

You can also delete copy by inserting the I-beam tool into a sentence, using the Delete key to backspace, removing copy from the blinking insertion bar backwards one letter at a time. Wherever the I-beam tool is located, if you type in new copy it will appear to the right of the blinking insertion bar, and if you delete copy, it will delete from the bar to the left.

To move and duplicate text

To move text, you must first Cut or Copy it to the Clipboard, a temporary, invisible storage place in the memory. Then you paste it from the Clipboard into its new position. If you Cut and Paste the text, you will delete it from its original position. If you Copy and Paste it, you will leave the text in its original position, and paste a copy of it in the new position.

To cut and paste text Highlight it and select Cut from the Edit menu (or type the keyboard shortcut, Command-X). Insert the I-beam tool where you want to paste the text, and select Paste (or Command-V) from the Edit menu.

To copy and paste text Highlight it and select Copy from the Edit menu (or type the keyboard shortcut, Command-C). Insert the I-beam tool where you want to paste the text, and select Paste (or Command-V) from the Edit menu.

Using cut or copy and paste can save you time by allowing you to duplicate and edit text rather than retype it from scratch. For example, the paragraph "To copy and paste text," above, is just a copy of the paragraph preceding it, with the word "copy" substituted for the word "cut," and the keyboard shortcut changed. **NOTE:** The commands cut, copy, and paste— and their keyboard shortcuts—are common to all Macintosh applications.

Formatting type

To format type (to apply font and style specifications to it) first type and save the text. Then, with the I-beam tool, select (highlight) the text you wish to format. Select only as much text as will be formatted in the same style. Unfortunately, you cannot group-select type (select more than one non-contiguous area of text), so you will have to select and spec one group at a time. For example, on this page each paragraph of body text between heads would be selected and formatted separately, and then each head selected and formatted separately.

TIP: To save time, first select all the text by inserting the I-beam tool anywhere in the text and typing Command-A (Select All command from the Edit menu, also common to all Mac applications). Spec the body text while all the type is selected. This puts a "base" spec on the whole document. Then you can go back, select each line of subhead, and spec the heads quickly as exceptions to the text spec. When a document is comprised primarily of text with just a smattering of heads, this speeds up the formatting considerably.

Selecting a font Highlight the type you wish to spec and choose a font from the Font menu by dragging down the menu to display the font choices available, scrolling down the menu until the desired font is highlighted. Release the mouse button while the desired font name is highlighted; the text will change to the selected font. The default font selection (the one the program automatically selects for you if you don't make another selection) is Geneva, a Helvetica clone.

Selecting a point size Highlight the type you wish to spec and choose a point size (from 7 to 72 points) from the Size menu by dragging down the menu to display the point sizes available, until the

desired size is highlighted. Release the mouse button. The highlighted text will change to the selected point size. If the point size you want does not appear on the pull-down menu, select Other (or type Command-Shift-O). A dialog box will appear in which you can select any point size from 2 to 500 points. The default point size is 12 points.

Selecting leading Again, highlight the type you wish to spec first. Select one of the icons in the top center of the window, underneath the ruler, that represent single-, one-and-a-half-, or double-

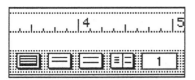

space (below, left). Or, if you wish to adjust the current line spacing, choose the last box on the right of that set, clicking on the left side to decrease the line spacing (or on the right side to increase the line spacing) of the currently selected type. The current spacing will appear in the box to the right of the increase/decrease spacing button. The default setting is preset for single-spacing, as shown above.

Selecting left/right alignment Highlight the type you wish to spec and choose an icon representing flush left, centered, flush right, or justified alignment from underneath the ruler; the text will change to the selected alignment. The default setting—shown above right—is flush left.

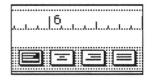

Selecting margins and indents Drag the arrow-point of the left margin icon under the ruler to set the lefthand margin. Drag the bar at its base to set a left paragraph indent. Drag the right margin arrow icon to set the right-hand margin. If you want flush left type with no paragraph indents, set the left arrow and its base at the same point on the ruler, as shown in the illustration on page 45.

The 'foot' or bar at the base of the left margin arrow sets the paragraph indent measure; the arrow itself sets the left margin. The righthand margin arrow sets the right margin measure.

To set tabs Drag a tab marker (one of the little triangles) from the tab wells in the gray bar underneath the ruler and place it anywhere between the margin markers that you want to put a tab indent. Repeat for as many tabs as you wish. You can also spec tabs numerically from a dialog box by selecting the Tab command from the Format menu.

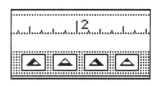

Creating custom styles MacWrite II has a new feature that lets you select and save entire styles (groups of formatting decisions) and name them. Select the command Custom from the Style menu (or type Command-D). A dialog box (shown on next page) will appear in which you may choose a font, point size, and style characteristics, name the entire set of choices, and add the style to the bottom of the Style menu. Named styles are automatically given keyboard shortcuts, such as 1, 2, etc., that, used in conjunction with the Command

Tabs markers can be pulled out of the tab wells, below, by dragging and placing them anywhere along the underside of the ruler— between the left and right-hand margins—that you want a tab to appear. The tab icons represent (left to right): left tab, centered tab, right tab, and decimal tab.

ABOUT WORD PROCESSING PROGRAMS

❙ **Single straight quote marks** are properly used to indicate the unit of measurement, feet.

❙❙ **Double straight quote marks** indicate inches.

' ' **Single curly quote marks** are used to enclose a quotation within a quotation. Right-hand curly quotes are used to indicate the possessive case of a noun or pronoun, or to indicate the omission of letters or figures.

" " **Double curly quotes** are true quotation marks, and are properly used to enclose all direct quotations, the titles of articles, chapters of a book and other compositions, or to place emphasis on a word.

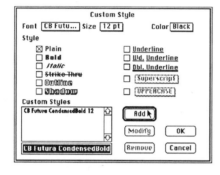

key, will apply the chosen style instantly to any currently highlighted text—a real time saver.

Formatting tips

Typing on the Mac is a little different from using a typewriter or doing typesetting. There are a few special tricks you can use to make your work look better and function better.

Hard and soft returns When typing in MacWrite, or any word-processing or page layout program on the Mac, let the lines "turn over" automatically when you reach the end of the line. This is called a "soft" return, and allows the lines to rebreak when the column width, or line length, is changed. Reserve using the Return key for the ends of paragraphs, when making lists of separate line entries, or wherever else you want a "hard" break to occur. Soft returns pick up the left margin indent specs, while hard returns pick up the paragraph indent specs.

Formatting for exporting If you're planning to export your file to a page layout program, where you'll do type formatting and page layout, keep your MacWrite document as simple as possible, using only the default settings for type fonts, style, point size, etc. Use only soft returns (see above) at the ends of lines, reserving hard returns for the ends of paragraphs and to separate line entries in lists. And don't use any paragraph indents; set everything flush left. Copy that is keyboarded this way is essentially without format

specs, and is easiest to select and spec within the page layout program: you don't have to undo anything before you start formatting. You can import preformatted files into page layout programs and change their specs, but they take more memory to store, more time to import, and time to undo—so why bother?

Spacing If you're used to typing on a typewriter, you probably put two spaces after periods and other punctuation marks. On the Mac, double-spacing interferes with proper formatting when type specifying, so learn to always type only one space after punctuation marks of any kind.

Smart versus dumb quotes One of the first telltale signs that a piece has been typeset by an amateur, and not a professional typesetter, is the use of straight (dumb) quote marks instead of the typographically correct curly (smart) quotes. Few people know that these marks are not interchangeable: single straight quote marks are correctly used to indicate measurements in feet; double straight quote marks indicate measurements in inches. Curly quotes, on the other hand, indicate quotation marks and apostrophes. Use the correct marks at the correct time (see sidebar at left) and make your work look professionally formatted.

Formatting quotes The key on the Mac keyboard that has the double and single quote marks types straight quotes only. Unfortunately, to get curly quotes, you must go to a little extra trouble:

' **For a left-hand single quote:** Hold down the Option key and press the right-hand bracket key ( ])

' **For a right-hand single quote:** Hold down both the Option and Shift keys, and press the right-hand bracket key ( ])

" **For a left-hand double quote:** Hold down the Option key and press the left-hand bracket key ([ )

" **For a right-hand double quote:** Hold down both the Option and Shift keys, and press the left-hand bracket key ([ ).

Chapter 7: Graphics

Graphics applications are the programs that you use to create illustrations and to draw charts and graphs. Most graphics programs are either bit-mapped, which means that you draw pictures dot by dot with *pixels*, or object-oriented, which means that you draw whole objects, such as lines, shapes, and curves. Pixels can be erased bit by bit; objects cannot be erased a bit at a time and must be deleted in their entirety. Bit-mapped drawings print out showing rough, pixelated edges. Object-oriented illustrations look like they were inked with a ruling pen, and print out as finely as the resolution of the output device on which they are printed.

Illustration by Max Seabaugh in SuperPaint

ABOUT GRAPHICS PROGRAMS

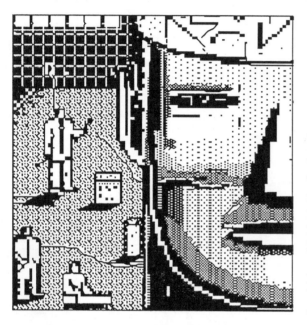

The illustration above, created in SuperPaint, takes full advantage of the aesthetic qualities of bitmaps that have been stretched and distorted.

Graphics applications are divided into two kinds of programs: painting or drawing.

Painting programs

are bit-mapped, or pixelated, which means that you create shapes and patterns dot by dot. In paint programs, you add or delete dots (pixels, bits) one at a time, and you can erase or edit images bit by bit. Pixelated programs were the first kinds of graphics applications available, and early programs like MacPaint and SuperPaint were black and white only. Today complex color pixelated programs such as SuperPaint 2, PixelPaint and Studio 8 allow you to truly paint in full color.

Drawing programs, on the other hand, are object-oriented, which means that you create whole objects—lines, shapes, etc.—at a time. In order to change them or edit them, you must change or delete the entire object. You cannot erase or edit pixels in an object-oriented program, because there are no pixels. The pixels you see onscreen are merely the screen representation (at about 72dpi) of smooth, non-pixelated objects. When you print out an image from an object-oriented program, it prints perfectly smoothly, as though you'd drawn it in pen and ink.

PostScript drawing programs (also sometimes called vector-based programs) use the mathematics of bezier curves to describe the path that a line or shape takes from its starting point to its end point, like drawing with french curves. Anchor points describe the beginnings and ends of lines, and the line or curve between them is called a path. Because shapes are described mathematically, they can be scaled, rotated, skewed, distorted, and manipulated in a number of ways.

Adobe Illustrator, FreeHand, and CricketDraw are all examples of object-oriented drawing applications based on the PostScript programming language. Other drawing programs like MacDraw are

also object-oriented, but based on other programming languages like QuickDraw. SuperPaint has both a paint and a draw layer, combining a taste of both methods of working in one application—although work done in one layer cannot be edited in the other layer: paint and draw data are not interchangeable.

Scaling and printing

PostScript images are completely scaleable: they can be infinitely enlarged or reduced either by scaling on-screen, or while printing, with no loss or distortion of detail or proportion. The files are device independent, which means that they will print as finely and smoothly as the capability of the output device that they are being printed on. Bit-mapped images tend to distort when scaled onscreen, but can be printed out—or imported into page layout programs—at enlarged or reduced sizes. Their tendency to distort can be used to advantage to create unusual artistic bit-mapped effects.

Stroking and filling

Shapes—whether bit-mapped or object-oriented—are outlines that can be stroked by selecting different line weights, pen patterns, and other line attributes, and filled by selecting different fill patterns and colors.

INTRODUCTION TO SUPERPAINT 2

SuperPaint is a versatile graphics application with two programs in one: drawing and painting.

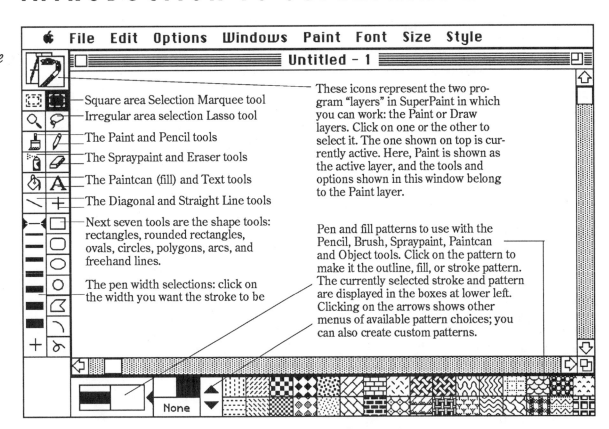

 File   Edit   Options   Windows   Paint   Font   Size   Style

Untitled – 1

—Square area Selection Marquee tool
—Irregular area selection Lasso tool

—The Paint and Pencil tools

—The Spraypaint and Eraser tools

—The Paintcan (fill) and Text tools

—The Diagonal and Straight Line tools

—Next seven tools are the shape tools: rectangles, rounded rectangles, ovals, circles, polygons, arcs, and freehand lines.

The pen width selections: click on the width you want the stroke to be

These icons represent the two program "layers" in SuperPaint in which you can work: the Paint or Draw layers. Click on one or the other to select it. The one shown on top is currently active. Here, Paint is shown as the active layer, and the tools and options shown in this window belong to the Paint layer.

Pen and fill patterns to use with the Pencil, Brush, Spraypaint, Paintcan and Object tools. Click on the pattern to make it the outline, fill, or stroke pattern. The currently selected stroke and pattern are displayed in the boxes at lower left. Clicking on the arrows shows other menus of available pattern choices; you can also create custom patterns.

None

SuperPaint's two layers

SuperPaint has two layers that you can work in. The Draw layer is object oriented: everything you draw is a complete object. You cannot work with or erase only part of an object, only the whole object. The Paint layer is bit-mapped. When you draw objects such as shapes and lines, you can manipulate them and add to or subtract from them bit by bit, and erase parts of them.

You can work in only one of these layers at a time, although you could use, say, a Draw layer background with a Paint layer foreground. Think of layers as being like overlays in regular pasteups: each layer has something different on it, but each is in perfect registration. **TIP:** Put a little dot in one corner of each layer to use as a registration mark when you print out your pages.

SuperPaint tips

The tips that follow are a brief introduction to using SuperPaint. Consult the manual for more specific user information.

Moving the page with the hand tool To eliminate the scroll bars to gain a larger working area, select Full Screen from the Window menu. Then, to call up a little hand that lets you move the page around without the scroll bars, hold down the space bar (the long bar in the center of the bottom row of keys). Use the hand tool to "slide" the page around inside the screen area.

To create mechanical color separations from a SuperPaint file: Create an illustration file for the base art, usually the black printer. Make a duplicate file using *Save As,* and name it for the color layer it will become, such as *Red Layer.* Select the entire illustration, and reverse it (turn it to solid black) by selecting the *Invert* command. Then delete all black areas not applicable to that color printer. Repeat for each color layer. For more detailed instructions, see "Mechanical or Spot Color Separations" on page 89.

Getting an enlarged view To call up an enlarged view of the area being worked on, select Fat Bits from the Options menu or double-click on the pencil tool. Repeat to bail out of the blown-up view. Fat Bits is useful when you want to draw or erase bit by bit: it shows an enlarged section of the illustration, and also shows the entire illustration in a tiny window so you can see the area you're working on in context.

Making copies Select the object to be copied by clicking and dragging around it with the Selection Marquee tool (selects a square chunk of the screen) or the Lasso tool (selects just the desired object, trimmed right up to its edges). Select Copy from the Edit menu (or Command-C) then select Paste from the same menu (or Command-V) and a new copy of the object will appear. It may show up directly on top of the original object; just drag it to wherever you want it to be.

To flip Select the object you wish to flip with the Selection Marquee tool, then select either Flip Horizontal from the Edit menu to make a mirror image of the object, or Flip Vertical to make the top and bottom trade places. You cannot flip a lassoed selection. You can reverse either kind of flip by repeating the command.

Undo and redo To undo your last move, select Undo from the Edit menu (or hit Command-Z). Your last move will be canceled out and you'll be back to where you were before you did it. You must decide immediately if you've made a mistake that you want to undo before you go on to your next move; later, you won't be able to undo.

You can toggle back and forth between Undo and Redo, if you want to think about it for a bit, but remember, once you've moved on, you can't go back with this easy bailout. You'll have to correct your mistake another way.

Constraining Constraining means to restrict the form of a shape while you are creating it by holding down the Shift key. Constraining with the Oval tool creates a circle, and with the Rectangle tool creates a square. Constraining painting or drawing tools such as the Line tool restricts them to vertical or horizontal movements.

Filling You can fill any shape or fully enclosed area with a pattern—on either a Paint or Draw layer—by "pouring" it in with the tip of the stream of paint from the Paint Bucket tool. Be sure no pixels are missing from the border of the shape you are filling or you will pour the pattern into the entire background. If that happens, immediately choose Undo from the Edit menu (or Command-Z). **NOTE:** A white fill pattern is opaque; fills of none are transparent (see below). **TIP:** You can also use fill patterns with the Spraycan tool, creating some interesting textures.

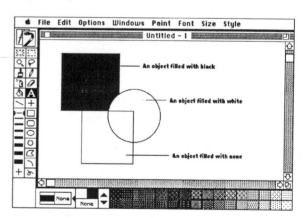

To stretch a shape Select the object you wish to stretch with the Selection Marquee tool, and drag on a corner of the object while holding down the Command key.

Plains Indian

Drawn in SuperPaint by Max Seabaugh. Note the use of Copy and Paste to repeat elements
like the feathers and brass tacks. Fill patterns are used to "color" the blanket stripes and gunstock
warclub. A white pencil has been used to scratch away the star-shaped patterns on the
shoulder and the texture of the buffalo fur hat.

SCANNING AND FILE FORMATS

Artist Illus2

Pickett icons

RAY 17.pict

Cabling.eps

Victorians.TIFF

Shown above, icons representing five of the most commonly used file formats for saving scanned art, or art that will be imported into page layout programs, from the top down: MacPaint, SuperPaint 2, PICT, EPS, and TIFF.

Scanning images

Scanners are input devices that enter two-dimensional visual data into the computer. Flat art is placed on a flat glass platen or run through a drum or roller, where it is read and interpreted as either line art or as digitized (pixelated) art. Three-dimensional images can be captured with video digitizers, which are essentially video cameras that read three-dimensional images, convert them into two dimensions, and record them in digital form using specialized software.

Using scanned images Scanned artwork like a pencil sketch can be used as is, in its rough, unedited form, or it can be cleaned up by editing its pixels in a paint program like MacPaint or SuperPaint. It can also be used as a template, or rough sketch, to trace over in a drawing program such as Adobe Illustrator. Line art can be scanned and saved as an object-oriented PICT file, for importation into a page layout program or for editing in MacDraw. Continuous tone black and white photographs can be scanned and used as position-only artwork, or brought into an image manipulation program such as Image Studio or Digital Darkroom, where they can be electronically retouched and used as final electronic art files within a page layout program.

Scanning text Special OCR (Optical Character Recognition) software can be purchased that will enable your scanner to read most typewritten—and some typeset—copy, saving you the necessity of rekeyboarding (retyping) the copy yourself.

File formats

Once you have created a scanned image you must save it in a file format appropriate for its intended use. If your scanning is done at a service bureau, be sure to tell them which of the following file formats to save your scan in.

MacPaint and SuperPaint

Sketches or other images scanned as bitmaps intended to be opened within paint programs should be saved as MacPaint files; these can be opened from within MacPaint, SuperPaint, Studio 8, or any other pixelated program, and then edited in black and white or converted—bit by bit—to color. MacPaint files can also be used as templates from within Adobe Illustrator: open Illustrator, and a dialog box will appear asking you whether or not you want to use a template. Scroll or drive until you find the name of the MacPaint file in the directory, then double-click to open it. The MacPaint image will appear grayed back onscreen; you can trace over it by hand using the Pen tool, or automatically using the Autotrace tool.

PICT Line art, when scanned, should be saved as a PICT file, a standard file format that can be used with many graphics programs and with any Post-Script printer. Scanned grayscale or color photos can be saved as PICT 2 files. PICT files can be opened and manipulated from within MacDraw or Super-Paint, or imported directly into any page layout program.

EPS Encapsulated PostScript is the file format used to save files drawn in Illustrator, FreeHand, and other PostScript drawing programs when you plan to import them into page layout programs. EPS files save grayscale and halftone screen data as well as a Macintosh screen image, and can print out on PostScript printers at full resolution.

TIFF and RIFF Tagged Image File Format and Raster Image File Format are used for saving grayscale images—scanned photographs that will be opened and edited within image manipulation programs such as Image Studio. Grayscale images use the capabilities of the color Mac IIs and color screens to display what appear to be continuous tone black and white photographs, which can be retouched electronically. New full-color image manipulation programs such as ColorStudio and Photo Shop are now available to edit color images, as well.

INTRODUCTION TO ILLUSTRATOR 88

Selection arrow
Hand tool
Zoom tool
Type tool
Freehand tool
Autotrace tool
Pen tool
Square tool
Circle tool
Blend tool
Scale tool
Rotate tool
Reflect tool
Shear tool
Scissors tool
Measure tool
Page tool

File Edit Arrange View Style Window

BAL/SHP/FINAL/2:BAL/SHP/SBG

Illustration above by Max Seabaugh in Adobe Illustrator.

About Illustrator
Adobe Illustrator is an object-oriented PostScript drawing program, which means that you create whole objects—lines, shapes, etc.—and in order to change them, you must change or delete the whole object. You cannot erase or edit the pixels you see onscreen, because they are merely the screen display of the PostScript image. When you print out an image from a PostScript program, it prints perfectly smoothly (limited only by the resolution of the output device), as though you'd drawn it in pen and ink.

Bezier curves
PostScript programs (also sometimes called vector-based programs) use a mathematical language of bezier curves to describe the path that a line or shape takes from its starting point to its end point. In Adobe Illustrator, these are referred to as anchor points and paths. Drawing with Illustrator is a little like drawing with french curves—you define a path first with anchor points, and then adjust the curve between them.

Viewing modes
When you work in Illustrator, you can either draw directly onscreen, or you can trace over a template. Templates can be useful when you want to scan a sketch or a photograph and use it as a starting point for your illustration. When you first open Illustrator, pull down the File menu and select New to create a new document window. A dialog box will apear, asking if you want to open a template. At this point you can choose a template by name from the directory, or click none.

When you are working in Illustrator, you can choose to view the template alone, your drawing superimposed over the template, the illustration alone, or a preview of the finished drawing. These options are available under the View menu.

When you select Template Only from the View menu, you'll see a grayed back image on screen: a MacPaint template that you can trace over.

Artwork Only from the View menu displays an outline representing the paths and anchor points in your drawing. Stroke and fill selections will not show up in this viewing mode.

When you select Preview from the View menu, you'll see a preview of your finished drawing, complete with stroke and fill selections.

Making templates If you want to scan an image to use as a template, ask your service bureau to save the scanned image as a MacPaint file. Or, if you wish, you can create a rough sketch directly in MacPaint and use it as a template. You might want to do this if you are more comfortable working in MacPaint; eventually, as you become more familiar with Illustrator, you'll find it more direct to sketch directly in that program.

Viewing sizes You may wish to change the size of the image as you work on it. To do so, click on the illustration with the Zoom tool (the little magnifying glass). To reduce the viewing size (to make the image smaller and see more of the page) select the Zoom tool, hold down the Option key, and click on the center of the image. Release the Option key. To enlarge the viewing size, select only the Zoom tool and click on the image.

The document always opens in 100% scale. Each time you click with the Zoom tool, it will enlarge or reduce by a factor of two, from 12.5% to 1600%.

Drawing with the Pen tool

To draw in Adobe Illustrator, you create paths, or lines, which are made up of one or more segments. Segments can be either straight lines or curves. The shape and size of a segment is determined by two anchor points at the beginning and end of the segment, and by direction points, which are like little handles with which you control the shape and length of the curve. Drawing is like playing connect-the-dots with a french curve: you determine where the anchor points should be placed, then rotate or pull on the direction point handles to adjust and refine the curve.

Kinds of paths There are two kinds of paths: open and closed. Open paths (below) are connected segments with two separate endpoints. Closed paths (below right) are loops of segments with no endpoints. Trying to fill an open shape can result in odd and unexpected results (shown, bottom) when viewing Artwork Only and when printing. Draw your line or shape first, then select it and choose stroke and fill attributes (next page).

The screen at right shows a template for two open paths made of several curved segments. Along each path you can see anchor points represented by small squares. The top path template has a drawing started, and shows an end point and its direction point and handle, and a second anchor point, also with a direction point and handles. By grabbing the handle of a direction point and pulling it, you can adjust the length, curve, and shape of the segment.

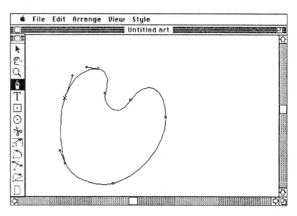

To draw a curved segment or path Select the Pen tool and position it where you want to begin the path. Press and hold down the mouse button, and drag—*away* from the direction that you want the curve to bulge—to create a direction point and handle for that first anchor point. Release the mouse button. Repeat to create the next anchor point (see example above). **TIP:** Position points on the sides of curves, not at the tops.

The curve at top left has been stroked with a black line and filled with none. The curve below left has been stroked with none and filled with black (both shown in Artwork Only view).

To adjust the shape of a curve There are three ways to adjust the shape of a curve once you've drawn it: you can drag a direction point to move the handle; you can drag the curve itself, and lengthen it or shorten it, or you can drag an anchor point, and move it a little. Each of these techniques will change the shape and length of the curve in slightly different ways. You may want to use all three to get the shape just right.

To draw a straight line Select the Pen tool, and position the pointer where you want to begin the line. Click and release the mouse button. Position the pointer where you want the line to end, and click again. Be careful not to drag while clicking, or you'll create direction points and end up with a curve instead of a straight line. To draw a perpendicular or horizontal line, hold down the Shift key between clicks to constrain (see page 52) the line.

To draw a closed shape Follow the instructions for drawing a curved path, and continue drawing curves until you have brought the shape around to the beginning. Position the pointer on the first anchor point in the path. When you close a path, the pointer changes to an x (shown above). If the pointer doesn't change to an x, it means the first anchor point and the last anchor point aren't in exactly the same position and the path hasn't closed. Try enlarging the view, then select Undo from the Edit menu and try again.

Corners and joins

Making sharp corners that change direction suddenly, and connecting straight lines with curves require special tricks:

To create corners in a curved path When you want to change direction sharply in the middle of a curved path, you'll need to create a corner point. To do so, draw your path up to the point where you want the corner point to occur, then hold down the Option key, click the pointer again on the same point, then click to create the next point in the path, and release the Option key (below). You can now continue in the new direction.

The arrow, left, is pointing to the corner point created by holding down the Option key and clicking again to change direction.

To join a straight line to a curve Hold down the Shift key while using the Pen tool to draw a perfectly straight line (the Shift key constrains the line to the perpendicular or horizontal). At the point where you want to make a transition from a straight line to a curve, create a corner point by holding down the Option key, then click again on the point you want to make into the corner point. Release the Option key (below). The corner point keeps the straight line from being affected by the direction handles of the curve next to it.

The corner point prevents the straight line from being affected by the curve next to it.

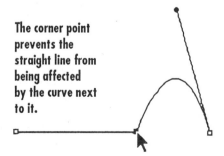

Stroking lines and filling shapes

Once you've drawn a line or shape you can select fill, stroke, and line weight specifications. These are available in a dialog box (shown below), reached by selecting Paint from the Style menu, or by typing Command-I.

To stroke an open path (a line) Select a Fill of none and a stroke of black, white, none, or any combination of process color tints. You can select the width of the line by typing in the desired weight in points in the box labeled Weight. You can select sharp or rounded line ends (caps) and corners (joins) by clicking the appropriate buttons under Caps and Joins. It's important to make sure not to select a fill for an open path, because Illustrator will fill the curves between and around the line, making a very odd, nonlinear effect (see example at bottom of page 57).

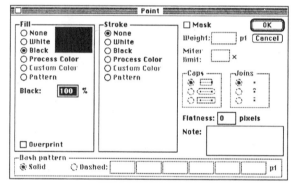

To fill a closed path (a shape) Select a Fill of black, white, none or any combination of process color tints and a stroke of black, white, none, or any combination of process color tints. Select a line width, as above. You can fill and stroke in the same or different tint selections, as shown below.

A closed path, filled and stroked with black

Stroked with black and filled with white or none

Stroked with black and filled with 20% black

When you select Paint from the Style menu, a dialog box appears in which you can select line strokes and weights, and fills for shapes.

A note about color viewing on the Mac: the colors you specify — whether process tints or PMS colors— are displayed onscreen as facsimile colors made up of red, green, and blue. They are not inks or pigment colors, but transparent colors, and so tend to appear lighter and brighter onscreen than in the final printed output.

A black and white drawing in Illustrator. Shapes filled and stroked with black are laid down first; shapes filled and stroked with white lay on top. Detail shapes and lines—both black and white—continue to layer on top of one another in the order in which they are drawn. You can select any object and move it to the top or bottom of the stack of objects by first cutting it (type Command-X) and then pasting it in front (type Command-F) or behind (type Command-B).

This inset shows the same illustration onscreen in the Artwork Only viewing mode (see page 56).

Illustration by Max Seabaugh in Adobe Illustrator

Tips: If you press the Command key while you're using any other tool, you'll get the selection arrow without having to leave the tool you're in. Releasing the Command key returns you to the tool you were in. This is useful for pausing to nudge a shape with the arrow while you're still in the process of drawing it, without interrupting the flow. Similarly, holding down the Command key and the space bar while you're using any tool gives you the magnifying glass tool, which you can click anywhere on the page to increase the size of the illustration without leaving the current tool. Holding down the Option and Command keys plus the space bar gives you the Reducing Glass tool.

To select an entire object or path Hold down the Option key while clicking anywhere on the path, or drag the selection arrow to create a selection marquee. When an entire object is selected, the anchor points will be solid black. If you've selected an object and its anchor points look like hollow squares, it is not fully selected and can't be moved. If you click on a path without holding down the Option key, you will select only that segment of the path. The selected segment's anchor points will be black; all others will be hollow.

To duplicate objects When you want to make multiples of shapes or paths instead of redrawing them, you can select them and duplicate them. Select the entire object with the pointer arrow or selection marquee (drag the selection arrow on the screen to capture the object inside a dotted selection box; this is called the selection marquee). Drag the object while holding down the Option key, and release the Option key after the object is in position. You can then select the copy with the pointer and reposition it if desired.

Special effects tools

Special effects tools let you resize, rotate, and flop objects, as well as create blends of shapes and/or colors. They all work similarly:

To resize an object, click on any point with the Scale tool while holding down the Option key. A dialog box will appear in which you can scale by percentage. Or, if you click on an object with the Scale tool without holding down the Option key, you can rescale manually by grabbing and dragging a corner or single point of the object.

To rotate an object, use the Rotation tool in the same manner described above.

To create a mirror image of an object, use the Reflect tool as described above.

To create a blend of one color to another, or a transition of one form to another (or both), use the Blend (Transformation) tool as follows:

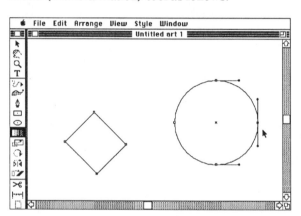

Create the shapes you wish to blend; then stroke and fill them. While they are still selected, ungroup them by typing Command-U. Hold down the Command and Option keys to get the pointer arrow, and click to select one point in each shape (as shown above). Click on each selected point with the Blend tool. A dialog box (below) will appear. Choose the number of steps in which you want the blend to occur, then click OK.

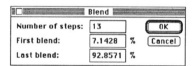

The wristwatch icon will appear during the time it takes to compute the blend, then an outline will appear representing the blended shapes (below).

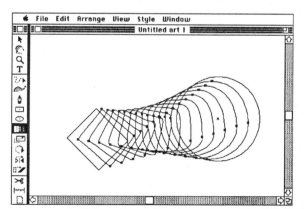

A combination of blends and masks: the blend in the eyewear, above, was masked out of the curved rectangle; see how the blend covers the entire area in the screen view, below. Because it has been masked, only the portion within the curved rectangle appears, left.

To see the actual blend (below), select Preview from the View menu. The example shows a 13-step transition between a 100% black square to a 10% black circle. You can use the blend tool to blend shapes, or tints (colors), or both.

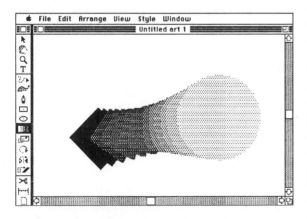

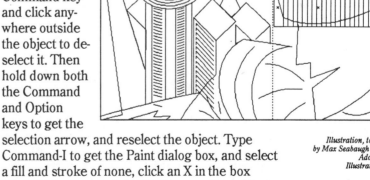

Illustration, top, by Max Seabaugh in Adobe Illustrator

To create a mask Any shape can be used as a window to mask out an area filled with a blend or a pattern. To create a mask, first create the blend or pattern that you want to fill the masking shape with. Then create the shape or object that you want to use as the mask itself, and, while it is still selected, type Command-U to ungroup it. Hold down the Command key and click anywhere outside the object to deselect it. Then hold down both the Command and Option keys to get the selection arrow, and reselect the object. Type Command-I to get the Paint dialog box, and select a fill and stroke of none, click an X in the box labeled Mask, and click OK. The masking object should still be selected; type Command-X to cut it, then select both the masking object *and* the blend or pattern together. Type Command-B to paste the mask behind the pattern. Select both the masking object and the pattern together again, then type Command-G to group them. Type Command-Y to preview the mask effect.

Adding and specifying type

To add type to an Illustrator file, select the Type tool and click with it where you want to place the type on the page. If you are going to center the type, put the pointer where you want the center of the line of type to be. If you are going to flush the type left or right, the pointer should be placed where you want the left or right end of the line to be. A dialog box will appear in which you can select a type font, the point size, leading, letter spacing, and alignment. Then type the text into the space at the bottom of the box.

Enter your text here by clicking in this space and typing on the keyboard. You can enter up to 255 characters at once in one text block, and they must all be in the same font, style, and size.

Tip: If you let the type turn over automatically in the box when it comes to the end of the line, the type on your page will be one long, continuous line. If you want the type to break in specific places, you'll have to use the Return key to indicate the end of one line and the start of the next line.

NOTE: The text feature in Illustrator isn't meant to be a complete word processing tool. It's intended for creating labels or short text blocks. If you need to enter a large block of text, or want complex type specs, consider importing your illustration into a page layout application and applying the text in that program. You'll have more control and will be able to specify more than one set of font specs per block of text.

To move type Once you've typed and speced your text, click OK to close the Type dialog box. The type will appear onscreen with an anchor point and baseline. If you want to move the type, select the anchor point with the selection arrow and drag to reposition it.

To edit type Select the type block with the selection arrow by clicking anywhere on its baseline. Type Command-T to call up the Type dialog box; you can change either the text or its specs from within the dialog box. Remember, all the type in any one text block must all be in the same font, style, and size. To change any of these specs, you must create a new text block with the Type tool.

About printing Illustrator

You can print an Illustrator file on any PostScript printer, and the clarity with which it is reproduced will depend on the resolution of the printer used. A black and white Laserwriter or a color QMS printer will print out paper output at 300 dots per inch (dpi), while typesetting-quality Linotronic and Compugraphic printers can print onto paper or film at well over 1200 dpi. A Macintosh service bureau can also create four color separations from your Adobe Illustrator file, using a program called Adobe Separator, and print them out onto negative film, from which matchprint or chromalin proofs can be made.

The drawing board metaphor Illustrator's page setup is based on the visual metaphor of a large sheet of drawing board divided into nine segments. You are usually working in the middle, or segment number 5. When you print an Illustrator document, tell the printer to print from page 5 to 5, not All or page 1 (enter these numbers in the Print dialog box under the File menu).

1	2	3
4	**5**	6
7	8	9

In Illustrator, you are usually working on page 5, so when you go to print, be sure to tell the printer to *print page 5*, not *page 1*. You can, however, draw and print on all 9 segments for oversized drawings.

Chapter 8: Page Layout

Page layout applications are the programs that you use to spec type and do page layouts and electronic pasteups. Some have sophisticated kerning, tracking, letter-spacing, hyphenation, spell-checking, grids or guidelines, and search and replace capabilities. You can type directly on the page using built-in word processing, or import text created in a program like MacWrite or Microsoft Word. You can import illustrations created in a graphics application or photos from a scanner. This is the place where you bring all the elements together and create complete page designs.

Illustration by Max Seabaugh in SuperPaint

ABOUT PAGE LAYOUT PROGRAMS

PAGE LAYOUT PROGRAMS

Page layout programs allow you to either create text directly in the program, or import it from a word processing program, and apply sophisticated type specifications and styling to the text. Graphic elements must be created in an illustration program and imported into the layout program, where they can be scaled, moved, and in some programs even rotated on the page, but not redrawn or edited.

Page layout programs allow you to either create text directly in the program, or import it from a word processing program, and apply sophisticated type specifications and styling to the text. Graphic elements must be created in an illustration program and imported into the layout program, where they can be scaled, moved, and in some programs even rotated on the page, but not redrawn or edited.

Page layout programs bring together files created in word processing, painting, and drawing applications. You combine them into one file, where you can rearrange the elements, scale the artwork, spec the type, and create an electronic page design. Complete "pasteups" can be printed out on a laser printer for proofing even before actual type has been set, making it possible to make corrections on final-looking pages before expensive type output has been ordered, or expensive production time has been spent. Final output can be on paper like a complete, one-piece pasteup; or on negative or positive film that you can send directly to the printer.

The leading programs

The leading page layout programs available today are all excellent, but each has its own style, capabilities, and some advantages—and disadvantages—compared to the others.

PageMaker The first and still most widely used page layout program, Aldus's PageMaker, is easy to learn and reliable, and has a flexible approach to placement and movement of objects on the page. A favorite among many graphic designers, it is popular and widely supported, but does not have the most advanced type specification or word processing capabilities.

Ready,Set,Go! and Design-Studio Letraset's programs Ready,Set,Go! and its new, professional-level big brother, DesignStudio, are equally simple to use but also provide far greater type control and accuracy, including professional support features such as type systems specifications ability, custom modular grids (as opposed to simple vertical columnar grids or guidelines), interactive facing page design, access to the entire Pantone Color Library for specifying the color of type and objects, kerning and tracking customization tables, and thumbnail sketch-size viewing and output. DesignStudio has added type rotation, circular and other odd-shaped text and picture blocks, an automatic fraction maker, and a pasteboard metaphor-based page setup similar to PageMaker's. Ready,Set,Go! and DesignStudio are not yet very well known, but certainly deserve to be. They combine the best features of PageMaker and Quark XPress: freedom of movement combined with a high degree of precision and control.

Quark XPress Quark XPress, like Ready,Set,Go! and Design-Studio, is less well-known than PageMaker. But it has advanced type control, word processing capabilities, and advanced color output capabilities, all of which make it attractive to professional publishers. The current version of Quark is rigid to use, tying text and graphics together in "frames," and does not allow users to work in an interactive facing page mode. A new version is in the works that should fix these drawbacks.

What program to choose? If you're just starting out, and want an easy-to-learn, widely used program that most output service bureaus are familiar with, you might want to start with PageMaker. But if you're a professional designer or publisher, DesignStudio and Quark XPress are by far the most sophisticated programs. They'll take a little longer to master, but you'll be able to produce professional-quality documents immediately and gradually grow into their more advanced features. Do keep in mind, as always when choosing software programs, the question of compatibility with your clients and co-workers, and support from your local service bureau.

INTRODUCTION TO READY,SET,GO! 4.5

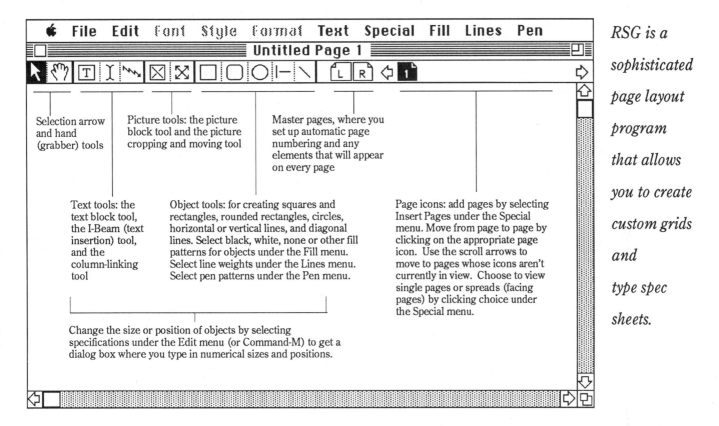

ᅥ File Edit Font Style Format Text Special Fill Lines Pen

Untitled Page 1

Selection arrow and hand (grabber) tools

Picture tools: the picture block tool and the picture cropping and moving tool

Master pages, where you set up automatic page numbering and any elements that will appear on every page

Text tools: the text block tool, the I-Beam (text insertion) tool, and the column-linking tool

Object tools: for creating squares and rectangles, rounded rectangles, circles, horizontal or vertical lines, and diagonal lines. Select black, white, none or other fill patterns for objects under the Fill menu. Select line weights under the Lines menu. Select pen patterns under the Pen menu.

Page icons: add pages by selecting Insert Pages under the Special menu. Move from page to page by clicking on the appropriate page icon. Use the scroll arrows to move to pages whose icons aren't currently in view. Choose to view single pages or spreads (facing pages) by clicking choice under the Special menu.

Change the size or position of objects by selecting specifications under the Edit menu (or Command-M) to get a dialog box where you type in numerical sizes and positions.

RSG is a sophisticated page layout program that allows you to create custom grids and type spec sheets.

About Ready,Set,Go!

Ready,Set,Go! is a sophisticated page layout program that allows you to easily create custom grids and page layouts, create type spec sheets for formatting type, import text files or create text directly on the page, import art files from popular graphics programs, and combine them all to create complete camera-ready artwork for printing on any PostScript printer. We recommend that you use version 4.5a or later, or you might see if you can find DesignStudio, RSG's new, professional-level older brother. DesignStudio works much like RSG, but because it is *so* new as of this printing, we'll show you Ready,Set,Go!

The basic document window—which lets you create and view multiple pages—and an explanation of the functions of the tools in the toolbar are shown above.

How to start

When you first open an RSG document, you will need to start by selecting various setting preferences. Select Preferences from the Special menu and click your preferred selections below:

Preferences

Units: Inches / Centimeters / Picas/Points

Guides

☒ Show Ruler
☒ Show Print Area
☒ Show Block Outlines
☒ Show Register Marks
☒ Show Color Names
☐ Disable Font Scaling
☒ Use Fast Halftones

Starting Page Number: 1
Auto Kern Threshold: 12.00 points
Auto Kern Scale Factor: 100 percent
Auto Line Spacing: 100 percent
Snap To Strength: 5 pixels
Greeking Below: 7.00 points
Fixed Tab Width: 1.000 ems

Cancel / OK

To make the ruler disappear, click off the Show Ruler box. Select your preferred unit of measurement in the pop-up menu next to Units. Starting Page Number indicates the first auto-numbered page in the file. Choosing a smaller number for Greeking will accurately display type in small point sizes onscreen.

You might want to set up your page dimensions in inches, the default setting, and then change to picas and points to create a grid. It's easy to switch back and forth from one unit of measurement to another; just go back to the Preferences dialog box and make your changes.

About viewing and page sizes

You can view and work with your page at several different sizes, no matter what size screen you're working on. Five viewing scales plus thumbnails are available under Views in the Special menu, or by typing the keyboard shortcuts shown after each view size:

- Size to fit (Command-1)
- Half size (Command-2)
- 75% size (Command-3)
- 100% or Actual size (Command-4)
- Double size (Command-5)
- Thumbnails (Command-6)

Single or facing pages You can view and work with your document a single page at a time, or as facing pages—spreads—by clicking Facing Pages under the Special menu on or off. If you can't see the entire spread at once due to screen size, use the Size to Fit viewing mode—handy for doing overall page layout. If you want to get in close to work on text, use Actual size or Double size. You can switch back and forth between single and facing pages at any time.

Changing page size The default setting for RSG pages is 8 $1/2$" x 11" vertical. You can choose other page sizes, change page orientation from vertical to horizontal, or create custom page sizes in a dialog box reached by selecting the Page Setup command under the File menu. To create custom page sizes, click the Other button, then type in any desired page dimensions under Width and Depth. RSG can create custom page sizes up to 99 inches square.

About printing

RSG can print to any PostScript printer. If you're printing on a Linotronic or Compugraphic, you can output tabloid-sized (11" x 17") pages. If you're printing on a LaserWriter, you're limited to an 8 $1/2$" x 11" page size, however, and if your page size is larger, you'll have to print out in smaller sections that are pieced together. This is called *tiling*, and is a printer option that you can select in the Page Setup dialog box.

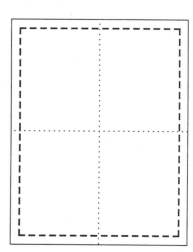

Tiling Tiling (above, right) automatically segments large, oversized pages into smaller pieces that the LaserWriter can print on 8 $1/2$" x 11" paper. You can specify the amount of overlap when you use tiling, and in order to make sure that it doesn't cut through your live matter, specify an extra-wide measure—perhaps 3 picas. You can then cut and piece together the entire page.

Scaling You can also print LaserWriter copies of oversized files in reduced scale for proofing, returning to 100% when printing final output on the Linotronic. To reduce the scale of the document for printing, select Printer Setup from the File menu, and type in the desired percentage of reduction. Tabloid pages will usually print out on letter-sized paper at a reduction of 65–70%.

Registration marks You can print out your pages complete with registration marks and color names if you wish. To do so, just click the appropriate boxes in the Page Setup dialog box under the File menu. Select the button Setup Marks and Names to enable you to pull color names and registration marks from the wells on the righthand side of the dialog box, and place them by hand wherever you want on the image of your page which will appear on the left-hand side of the dialog box.

If you're using an earlier version of the program, you can create handmade registration marks, as above, using the circle and line object tools (see example, opposite page). Later versions create them for you automatically.

11/6/90 FILE NAME: 7 OZ ROASTED US ALMONDS CAN LABELS

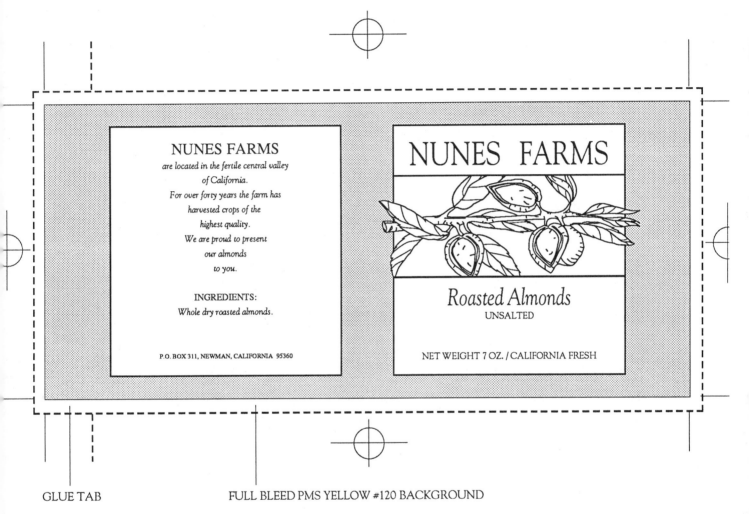

NUNES FARMS

are located in the fertile central valley
of California.
For over forty years the farm has
harvested crops of the
highest quality.
We are proud to present
our almonds
to you.

INGREDIENTS:
Whole dry roasted almonds.

P.O. BOX 311, NEWMAN, CALIFORNIA 95360

NUNES FARMS

Roasted Almonds
UNSALTED

NET WEIGHT 7 OZ. / CALIFORNIA FRESH

GLUE TAB   FULL BLEED PMS YELLOW #120 BACKGROUND

Illustration by Changhwan Kim in Adobe Illustrator; mechanical art-work in Ready,Set,Go!

Use Ready,Set,Go! to create complete mechanicals for camera-ready artwork, including crop marks, keylines and bleeds (created with the rectangle tool and a dotted line stroke), registration marks, rules, type, and imported illustrations. The registration marks shown here were created using the circle and line tools in RSG 4.0; RSG 4.5 and DesignStudio have automatic registration marks and color name placement available in the Page Setup dialog box. The date, file name, job name, and instructions to the printer can all be included in separate text blocks elsewhere on the page, as shown above.

Master Pages

Master Pages is a feature that allows you to create the equivalent of "base art": artwork that appears on every page in the same position. This is handy for elements such as folios (page numbers) or graphic elements such as rules.

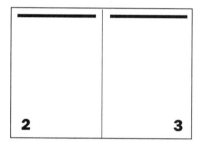

Use Master Pages to set up folios or graphic elements like header rules that appear on every page.

Automatic page numbering ensures that when you add, delete, or move pages in your document, all the pages will be renumbered automatically in sequence, starting with the page number that you specify as the starting page number in the Preferences dialog box.

You can create Master Pages for left-hand and right-hand pages, but you can have only one set of Master Pages per document. You can turn them on or off for each page in the document that you create, by clicking the Use Master command under the Special menu. It's best to use them for the bulk of your text pages, and turn them off for special pages such as chapter openers, or any other pages where you don't want the Master Page elements to appear. To control pages on a spread separately, first turn off Facing Pages in the Special menu, then turn Master Pages on or off for each individual page.

You cannot use Master Pages to create text blocks; these must be created on each page.

SHORTCUT: Set up one page (not in Master Pages) and duplicate it by selecting the command Insert Pages under the Special menu. A dialog box will appear in which you can create *x* number of new pages. The duplicate pages will have text blocks in the same position on each page. Any text blocks created in this way will be empty and ready to receive text. They will not be linked, however, until you have manually linked them with the linking tool.

Automatic page numbering One of the best uses for Master Pages is for setting up automatic page numbering. To do this, create a text block on each of the Master Pages (left and right) where you want the folios to appear. Click inside the text block with the I-beam tool, hold down the Command, Option, and Shift keys simultaneously, and type the number 3. Two pound signs (##) will appear in the text block, which are place-holders for your folios. Select these with the I-beam tool and apply your font and style specifications (see page 71).

If you are working on a very long project like a book, and are creating several files that you want to number sequentially, you can select what the starting page number should be for each separate file. Select Preferences from the Special menu, and a dialog box will appear in which you type the desired starting page number for that file. Each file in the series can start with a different page number.

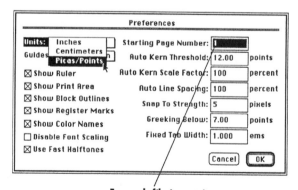

For each file in a string of sequentially numbered files, type in a new starting page number here. The page number icon in the tool bar at the top of the document window will correspond to the page number you specify here.

Chapter 1: Getting Started

What is a User Group?
Who are Apple's User Groups?
Why does Apple support User Groups?
What do User Groups do?

Apple creates, manufactures, and markets computers for a simple reason: so people can use them to make their life better. Our customers remain foremost in our minds. There is no upper limit to the quality of the products and service that we want to provide.

At Apple Computer, Inc., we strive to understand our customers' needs —to enhance their use of Apple products, to be courteous and instructive. As a corporate citizen, Apple wishes to be an economic, intellectual, and social asset in the communities in which it operates.

But beyond that, Apple expects to make this world a better place to live. We build products that extend human capability, freeing people to achieve more than they could without our products. We think of our products as enabling technology— technology that allows people to develop their abilities to the fullest.

Just Add Water is an extension of that company view. No matter how easy our computers are to use, the need for education will never go away. In fact, the need for support grows critically more important as our user base increases. One of the most beneficial avenues for user-to-user support has been at the grass roots level in the form of User Groups.

What is a User Group?

Apple defines a User Group as an affiliation of Apple users dedicated to enhancing the use of their Apple systems by sharing information, support, and insights with each other.

This is an intentionally broad definition. Apple User Groups exist for every product Apple has ever made, and for every application in which these products are being used. A User Group might reside in a corporation, government agency, university, or professional association, a school system, a national affiliation, or in a residential community.

What do all of these diverse groups have in common—the thing that makes them an Apple User Group? Answer: their educational objective. User Groups act as educational forces exploring information

An example of a page layout from a book in which all the page numbers, rules, and boxes outlining the page were created on the Master Pages. The gray box is on the bottom layer, and is covered by a white-filled box. Text blocks, the drop shadow box, and the rule box surrounding the illustration were created directly on the page.

The Grid Setup dialog box, far right, allows you to specify margin widths at the top, bottom, inside, and outside (or left and right edges) of the page; to select the amount of spacing between rows and columns; and to select the number of rows (horizontal grid modules) and columns (vertical grid modules) on the page. Click double-sided if your design is meant to print on both the front and back of each page. Note that you create a page grid from the outside in, by specifying margins, columns, and rows, and the spaces between them, and not by specifying the width of the columns themselves, as you may be accustomed to doing when drawing grids conventionally.

Creating and using grids

Ready,Set,Go! uses a grid-based page layout system that allows you to select from eight pre-made grids or create custom grids of any specification. To choose from the pre-made grids, select Design Grids under the Special menu. A dialog box will appear (see below) in which you can select from any of the existing grid choices; or you can click the Grid Setup button, which will call up a dialog box (above right) where you can alter an existing grid or create an entirely new one by typing in new specs.

Special
Facing Pages	⌘E
Size To Fit	⌘1
Half Size	⌘2
75% Size	⌘3
✓Actual Size	⌘4
Double Size	⌘5
Insert Page(s)...	
Delete Page(s)...	
Go To Page...	
Preferences...	
✓Snap To	
✓Use Master	
Design Grids...	**⌘9**
Alignment...	

To alter a grid setup: Type in new numbers specifying the measurements for top and bottom page margins, left/right or inside/outside page margins, the amount of spacing between horizontal rows or vertical columns, and the numbers of rows and columns. If you only want vertical columns without horizontal rows, enter the number 1 in the box labeled Number of Rows.

Design Grids

○ 1 х 1   ○ 5 х 5
○ 2 х 2   ○ 6 х 6
○ 3 х 3   ○ 7 х 7
○ 4 х 4   ○ 8 х 8
◉ Grid Setup

[OK]   [Cancel]

Left/right versus inside/outside If the box labeled Double Sided is checked, you will be able to specify measurements for inside and outside margins, as in a mirror-image grid. If Double

Grid Setup

Measurements In Picas.Points:

Top:	4.01	Bottom:	4.01
Inside:	4.00	Outside:	4.00
Row Spacing:	1.06	Column Spacing:	1.06
Number of Rows:	5	Number of Columns:	5

☒ Double Sided   [OK] [Cancel]

Sided is not checked, you will be able to specify left and right margin measurements, as for an asymetrical grid.

TIP: After you've typed the number in a box (field), press the Tab key to jump quickly from field to field within the dialog box.

Units of measurement The unit of measurement (indicated under the title Grid Setup) will be whatever choice is currently selected in the Preferences dialog box. To change the unit of measurement, go back to Preferences and reset.

The Snap To feature Once your grid is made, all objects will snap to the grid as they are created if the Snap To feature, available under the Special menu, is turned on. Or ignore the grid by turning Snap To off. Turning off Show Grid under the Special menu will turn off the grid, and with it the Snap To feature. Snap To is handy to use when you're creating text or picture blocks and want to quickly place them on the grid; later, if you want to resize or reshape the blocks, turn Snap To off and you'll be able to make changes independent of the grid. Whenever you create a new grid, Snap To is automatically on until you turn it off. You can also toggle it on and off from the keyboard using the shortcut Command-Shift-N.

Working with text

When you work with text in Ready,Set,Go!, you must first create special shapes, or text blocks, which define the area in which the text can be typed. Inside the text blocks, you are essentially inside a little word processing program. Outside the text blocks, you are in an object-oriented program where all objects themselves (such as text or picture blocks), after being created with their special tools, are selected, resized, moved, and deleted with the selection arrow tool. Inside the text blocks, you use the I-beam tool to enter, select, cut and copy, paste, delete, and spec text.

To create a text block Click and drag with the text block tool (the first tool in the text tool series) to create text blocks of any size you wish. They can snap to the grid or not, depending on your preference.

Selecting, moving, and resizing text blocks After you have created a text block, you must first select it with the arrow tool before you can move it or resize it. Select the block by clicking in the center of the block with the arrow. A selected block will be highlighted with little boxes at each corner and in the center of each side. If you want to move a text block, click in the center of the block and, holding the mouse button down, drag it to reposition it. If you want to resize a text block, turn Snap To off, then grab any one of the little selection boxes (handles) and drag to pull it in any direction. Grabbing corner handles enables you to pull diagonally; grabbing top or side handles enables you to pull up and down or sideways. You can also resize text blocks by typing in new numerical specifications in the Style Specifications dialog box (see page 72).

To link text blocks in a chain Use the linking tool (the one that looks like a lightning bolt) to connect any text columns you want to link in a chain. Click only once in each text block, and in the order in which you want the columns linked.

You can skip over columns or even skip to another page, but be sure to click only once—firmly—in each column. You can connect text blocks anywhere within a document, but you can't link text from one file to another. A good test of whether or not you have successfully linked text columns is to insert the I-beam tool in the last text column in the chain: the I-beam tool should jump to the beginning of the first block in the chain, indicating that the link was successful.

Importing text If you have a MacWrite, Microsoft Word, or other text file that you want to import, first make sure the file is free of all font and style formatting (see page 48). Insert your I-beam tool in a text column and select Get Text from the File menu. A dialog box will appear where you select the file you wish to import. In more recent versions of RSG, there is a box within that dialog box where you can click to automatically convert all straight quotes to curly, or smart, quotes. Wait until the text is finished pouring in before you start to format it.

Formatting text With the I-beam tool, highlight the text you want to format, then select a font from the Font menu, and a style (usually plain) and size from the Style menu (right). If the point size you want isn't shown, select Other and type the size you want in the dialog box that appears. Point sizes can be entered to two decimal points. Next, select flush left, right, centered or justified alignments from the Format menu. Select line spacing (leading), also under the Format menu, to specify desired line leading. Line spacing can also be specified to up to two decimal points.

Other formatting specs, such as indents, word or paragraph spacing, kerning or letterspacing, can be typed into dialog boxes by first selecting the text, then choosing the appropriate command from the Format menu.

Style
- ✓Plain ⌘P
- **Bold** ⌘B
- *Italic* ⌘I
- Underline ⌘U
- Outline
- Shadow
- Condense
- Extend
- Overstrike

- 9 Point
- ✓10 Point
- 12 Point
- 14 Point
- 18 Point
- 24 Point
- 36 Point
- Other...

Font
- ▲
- B Univers 65 Bold
- BI Bodoni BoldItalic
- Blk Univers 75
- BlkO Univers 75 BlackOblique
- BO Univers 65 BoldOblique
- Bodoni
- C Univers 57 Condensed
- CB Helvetica Condensed Bold
- CB Univers 67 CondensedBold
- CBO Univers 67 CondBoldObl
- Century Old Style
- Chicago
- CL Helvetica Condensed Light
- CL Univers 47 CondensedLight
- CLB Helvetica Condensed Black
- CLBI Helvetica Condensed BlackObl
- CLI Helvetica Condensed LightObl
- ▼

Tip: If any of the RSG dialog boxes get in your way onscreen, just grab them (using the selection arrow) on the gray bars at the top and move them. If they don't have a gray bar, they can't be moved.

Kerning and tracking Kerning is deleting space between pairs of letters to improve the appearance of the spacing between them. Tracking, on the Macintosh, means deleting space between several pairs of letters, to tighten up the spacing in a whole word, line, paragraph, or block of type.

To kern a pair of letters Select the right-hand letter of the kerning pair, select Kern from the Format menu, and type in the amount of space you want to delete between the pair, to three decimal points. Preview your selection by clicking Apply, then change it if desired. When you're pleased with the result shown onscreen, click OK to permanently apply your selection.

Tracking Tracking is similar to kerning, but encompasses anywhere from three or more letters, to whole words, lines, paragraphs, or text blocks. Whatever is selected will be tightened up by the amount you specify in the dialog box. As with kerning, preview your selection by clicking Apply and when it is correct, click OK.

Formatting shortcuts with style sheets
Style sheets are shortcuts that enable you to select all your type specifications from one dialog box, instead of pulling down many different menus. Once created, these styles can be applied to any selected text using keyboard shortcuts.

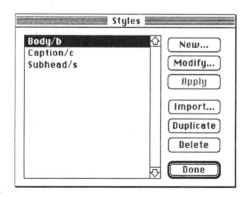

To import styles from another document, click the button Import. A dialog box will appear where you can find and double-click on the file with the styles you want to import. Note: You can't import from a currently open document. You can save time creating new styles by Duplicating and Modifying existing similar styles.

To create a style sheet Select the command Styles from the Text menu (or type Command-H). A dialog box will appear from which you can create new styles, and view, modify, duplicate, and delete existing styles. The box (below, left) already includes three styles that have been created, and that appear in the directory on the left side of the dialog box.

To create a new style Click New. A Style Specifications dialog box (above) will appear. In the box under Style Name, type in a name for this style. To be able to use a keyboard shortcut to apply this style, type a slash and a single letter abbreviation after the style name; for example: Body/b; Subhead/s; Caption/c; Title/t; Numbers/n.

Selecting from pop-up menus Click on the box next to Font; a pop-up menu will appear (shown above, covering Font), which you scroll down until you can select the font you want. Do the same for the point size, alignment, and hyphenation directories underneath. If you don't see the point size you want, select Other at the end of the menu and type any point size to two decimal points in the dialog box that appears. Click any box under Style to select styles other than plain.

Specifying spacing and indents On the right hand side of the Style Specifications dialog box are boxes where you can enter specs for word, line and paragraph spacing, and for paragraph, left, and right indents.

To specify spacing After word spacing, select 100%, unless you clicked the Condensed box under Styles, in which case type in 80%. After line spacing, type in the number of points of line leading you want to two decimal points. If you plan to use a full carriage return space between paragraphs, type 0 under paragraph spacing. If you want a half line space between paragraphs, divide the number of points of line leading you specified in two, and put that number under paragraph spacing.

To specify indents If you plan to use a full carriage return between paragraphs, you may want to enter a paragraph indent of 0. If you plan to use no extra vertical space between paragraphs, you'll probably want to enter a paragraph indent amount; a good rule of thumb is to use an indent amount equal to the point size of the type you're using. For example, with 9 point type you might spec an indent of .09, or 9 points. The first line in every paragraph will indent by that amount. The computer reads every carriage return created with the Return key as the start of a new paragraph, so don't use the Return key just to send a word down to the next line, or you might accidentally create a paragraph where you didn't intend one. The left indent entry will indent every line other than the first line of the paragraph by the specified amount, and right indent will indent that amount from the right.

To specify type color Click on the box labeled Set Color. A dialog box will appear in which you can scroll through a menu of all the Pantone colors; clicking on a color will enter it into the color swatch box in the upper right-hand corner of the dialog box. Clicking OK will apply that color to all type to which you apply this style

sheet. A shortcut for selecting a Pantone color, if you already know its number, is to enter the color number in the box just beneath the color swatch box and type a period after it; for example, typing 485-period will enter PMS Red #485 into the swatch box. Click OK to exit the dialog box.

Click OK when all selections have been made, and Click Done to exit the Styles box.

To apply styles Once you have created a style and named it, apply it to any highlighted text by typing Command-H to call up the Styles dialog box, then click on the desired style name, click Apply and then Done. Or use this keyboard shortcut technique: select the text, hold down the Command key, then type H and the single letter abbreviation after the style name. For example, typing Command-H-b would apply the style "Body." Once a style is applied to a block of type, any future changes to that style specifications dialog box will automatically be carried out on any text tied to that spec. To view or modify any style spec dialog box, select Modify in the Styles dialog box. Enter your changes in the Styles Specifications dialog box, then click OK to exit.

TIP: If you are planning to use one style spec— for example, body text style—for the bulk of the text in a document, select all of the text at once by entering the I-beam tool anywhere in the linked chain of text blocks and typing Command-A. When all of the text is thus selected, apply the style to all of the selected text. This sets up a base style spec from which you can then highlight and spec exceptions one line or block of type at a time, and apply the other style specs appropriate to them. This should speed up applying style specs in a long document. Remember, you can't group select noncontiguous lines of text on the Mac, so each style must be applied to each section of type individually.

You'll probably want to develop and use some standard keyboard shortcut names of your own, but here are a few ideas to get you started (note that the names are case sensitive; you can use both upper and lower case letters to signify different names):

Title/t
Subtitle/s
Byline/y
Level 1 head/1
Level 2 head/2
Level 3 head/3
Level 4 head/4
Intro text/I
Body text/b
Italic body text/i
Captions/c
Callouts/C
Notes/n
Dingbats/d
Bullet boxes/B

Working with objects

Ready,Set,Go!, like Adobe Illustrator, is an object-oriented program. All shapes that you create, like text blocks, picture blocks, circles, lines, rectangles, etc., are objects, and can be filled, stroked, duplicated, moved, layered, and scaled. To fill, stroke, move, resize, or work with an object in any way, you must first select it with the selection arrow. (Text itself, however, is not an object, and is always selected and worked on with the I-beam tool.)

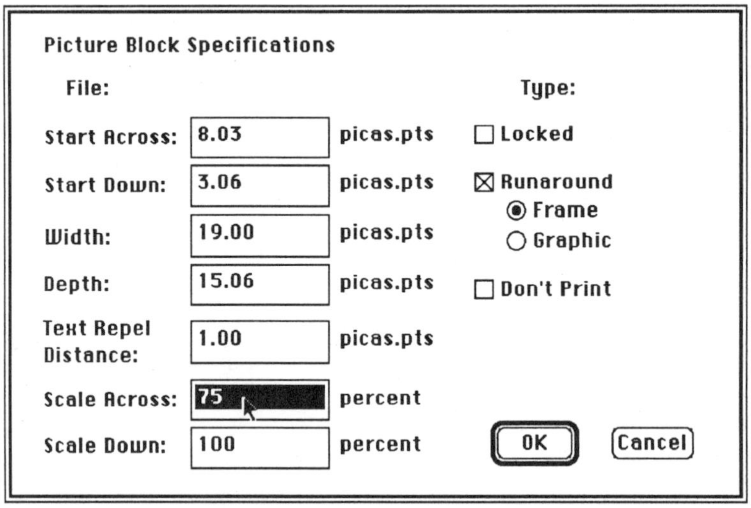

```
┌─────────────────────────────────────────────────────┐
│ Picture Block Specifications                          │
│   File:                                  Type:        │
│ Start Across:  [8.03    ]  picas.pts   ☐ Locked       │
│ Start Down:    [3.06    ]  picas.pts   ☒ Runaround    │
│                                          ● Frame       │
│ Width:         [19.00   ]  picas.pts     ○ Graphic    │
│ Depth:         [15.06   ]  picas.pts   ☐ Don't Print  │
│ Text Repel     [1.00    ]  picas.pts                  │
│ Distance:                                             │
│ Scale Across:  [75      ]  percent                    │
│ Scale Down:    [100     ]  percent    ( OK ) (Cancel) │
└─────────────────────────────────────────────────────┘
```

Selecting multiple objects To select more than one object at the same time, you can use one of these two standard methods:

1) Shift-clicking First, select one of the objects by clicking on it with the selection arrow. Then press and hold down the Shift key. Continue to click with the arrow on the rest of the objects that you want to include in the selection group. When you are through selecting, release the Shift key. All the selected objects will have handles, indicating that they are selected. They can now be moved or acted upon as a group.

This method is best used when you are trying to select a group of objects that are not necessarily placed in proximity to one another. If an element is accidentally selected in this manner, or you change your mind and want to remove one from the selection group, click on it a second time while the Shift key is still held down, and it will be deselected.

2) The selection marquee Click the selection arrow just outside the upper left-hand corner of the group to be selected, and, holding the mouse button down, drag the arrow to encompass the entire group. A dotted rectangle, called a *selection marquee*, will appear and surround the selected

objects. When you release the mouse button, all the selected objects will have handles, indicating that they are selected.

This method can be used only when all the objects to be selected as a group are in proximity to one another, and other objects are not interspersed with them.

Resizing an object When you want to resize an object, select it, grab one of the handles that indicate that it's selected, and drag in the direction that you want to resize. Or, if you want to make an object an exact size, select it, type Command-M to call up its Specifications dialog box, and type in new dimensions after Width and Depth (see the dialog box above).

Locking an object Sometimes you might want to "lock" an object so that it cannot be moved or altered accidentally. To do so, first select the object with the selection arrow, then select Lock from the Edit menu. To work with the object, be sure to first unlock it by selecting Unlock from the Edit menu. You can also lock and unlock an object in its Specifications dialog box (see above).

To see the placement, size, scale, or other specifications of any selected object such as a rule, a picture block, or a text block, double-click on the object, or select the object and then select the command Specifications from the Edit menu, or type Command-M. The dialog box shown at left will appear. In it, you can change or specify where the object starts on the page, from the top down and from left to right; its width and depth; the distance you want it to repel from nearby text (runaround); its scale across (width) or down (height); whether it is locked or not; whether runaround is on or off, and runs around the graphic shape or its frame; and finally, whether the object should print or not.

Using cut and paste You're already familiar with using Command-X or -C and Command-V to cut or copy and paste. In RSG, these commands are real time-savers if used creatively: you can use them to copy selected objects from other RSG files by opening two RSG documents at the same time and cutting or copying and pasting between them. You can create objects on one page and copy them to another page in the same document. You can use copying as a shortcut to format type, by copying formatted text from one block into another block, deleting the text and retyping new text in the same block, which will then carry the specs of the previous type in that block.

Working with layers In RSG, you can create objects that overlap one another such as text or picture blocks and rules or shapes. The most recently created object will always be on top of the previously created objects. If you find that you can't seem to select a particular object or get to it, that probably indicates that the object you're trying to select is underneath another object. For example, if you try to insert the I-beam tool into a text block that is behind another text block, the top text block will become active, preventing you from being able to place the I-beam in the block beneath. To get to the lower block, you must first bring it to the front. Select the topmost block (or object) with the selection arrow, and choose Send Behind from the Edit menu. That block is now beneath the other. The topmost block is now the active block, and you should be able to insert the I-beam tool and proceed.

Keyboard short-cuts can also be used to send a selected object behind another object (type Command-minus) or to bring it to the front (type Command-plus).

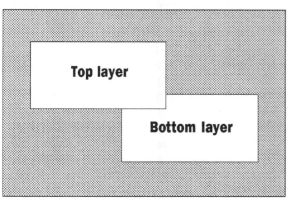

Picture Block Specifications dialog box showing:
File:
Start Across: 8.03 picas.pts
Start Down: 3.06 picas.pts
Width: 19.00 picas.pts
Depth: 15.06 picas.pts
Text Repel Distance: 1.00 picas.pts
Scale Across: 75 percent
Scale Down: 100 percent
Type: Locked, Runaround (Frame/Graphic), Don't Print
OK Cancel

Top layer
Bottom layer

Aligning objects You can align objects in two ways. The first is to group select all the objects that you wish to align with the selection arrow, and choose Alignment from the Special menu. A dialog box will appear in which you can specify whether you want them to align at their tops, bottoms, or sides.

The second way to align objects is by specification. Select an object with the selection arrow, and type Command-M. A dialog box will appear in which its location on the page is specified by Start Across and Start Down. Note these two positions and close the dialog box. Select the second object, type Command-M again, and enter the same specification for either Start Across (to align horizontally) or Start Down (to align vertically).

You can copy the coordinates from the Specifications dialog box of one object in order to place another object at exactly the same starting position horizontally or vertically.

Don't print If you want to create an object on the screen that you do not wish to have print when you output the file (such as a box indicating a trim edge for a page size smaller than standard, or a detail that you want to print in a second color), first select the object with the selection arrow, type Command-M to get its Specifications dialog box, then click the box that says Don't Print.

Duplicating This is an easy way to copy objects accurately. For example, suppose you want to create a form that has a hairline rule between each line of type, for filling in information. Instead of creating each rule separately, try this:

1 **Create a text block, enter and format the type. Note the line leading.**
2 **Create one rule of the desired width, and, using the selection arrow, select and move it into position above your first line of type.**
3 **While it is still selected, type Command-D. A dialog box (shown above) will appear asking how many duplicates you want. Type in the number of rules you want to add.**
4 **Type 0 for Horizontal Offset.**
5 **Then type in whatever the amount of your line leading is (in points) for Vertical Offset. For example, if you are using 9 point type with 20 points line spacing, type in .20, then click OK.**

The correct number of rules will appear, accurately placed the same distance beneath each line of type, and exactly aligned horizontally.

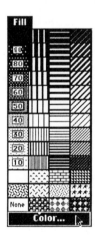

Filling and stroking objects Objects created with the object tools can be outlined and filled with various pen and fill patterns from the Fill, Lines, and Pen menus (the Fill menu is shown, left) either when they are created or selected. You can combine selections from these menus; for example, if you want a finer dotted line than the one available in the Lines menu, select a vertical stripe from the Pen menu and draw a horizontal line. It's as though you've filled your pen with dotted ink. You can select fill and pen colors by clicking on the box labeled Color at the bottom of the menu; select a PMS color in the same way that you select color type (see page 73 and "Color menus," below). Any color can be combined with any of the screen tints or patterns in the Fill menu to create color tints or patterns.

Color menus At the bottom of the Fill, Pen, and Text menus, you will find a box labeled Color, which leads to a Color Selector dialog box (see right). If you are using a black and white computer, the selections will appear in B&W screen tints as shown, with the Pantone color

name and/or number surprinted. If you are using a color monitor, the colors appear in color. Drag down the menu, then click on any color bar to make a sample of that color appear in the swatch box at the upper right. Or, if you know the PMS color number you want to select, type it in the box directly beneath the color swatch box and type a period after it. That color will appear. To color an object, rule, or text, first highlight the object or text, then select a color from this dialog box and click OK to exit.

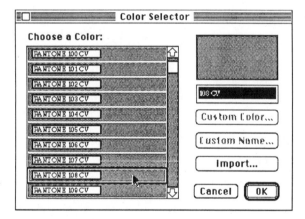

Custom colors You can customize the first twenty colors in the palette (with the exception of red, black, and white) and the new palette will be saved with the document in which it was created. To customize a color, select it, then click the Custom Color button (shown above). If using a color monitor, select a new color, preview it onscreen, and name it. On a B&W monitor, type in percentage values for Red/Green/Blue color specifications, and when you have specified the color desired, click OK, then select the Custom Name button and name your new color.

Importing color palettes Once you've created a custom palette in one RSG file, you can import it into another document. To do so, select Color from the Text, Fill, or Pen menus, click Import, find the other RSG file with the palette you want to import, and double-click on its name. **NOTE:** You cannot import from a currently open file.

DESKTOP DESIGN

*Computer-aided design and
production for graphic designers*

For Macintosh Plus, SE, and II Users

An example of a black and white cover comp created in RSG, with graduated screen tint artwork and a black and white illustration, both created in Adobe Illustrator, saved as EPS files, and imported into RSG picture blocks. Rectangles filled with a solid black fill pattern were used to create the black boxes under the title and at the lower left edge of the cover; and a rectangle filled with a 10% tint of black and stroked with a 1-point black rule indicating the trim edge is underneath all.

The two picture blocks above contain the same art file, cropped and sized differently. The top image is scaled at 100%, the bottom image at 200%.

Working with picture blocks

Picture blocks are objects, just like text blocks, that are created with a special tool—the picture block tool—and then activated with a cropping tool to receive (import) pictures that were created in graphics programs and then saved in special file formats (see page 54). The Cropping tool is also used to grab and slide pictures around inside picture blocks. To move, resize, or work with the picture block itself in any way after it has been created, rather than the graphic inside it, you must use the arrow tool.

To create a picture block Use the Picture Block tool (the first tool in the picture tools series) and drag to the size you want. Next click inside the picture block with the Cropping tool (the second picture tool). A pattern will appear that signifies that the block is ready to receive a picture. Select Get Picture from the File menu. When the directory window appears, double-click on the name of the picture you want to open, or "drive" to another disk to find another picture. The picture will appear at 100% in the picture block.

To scale a picture Select the picture block with the selection arrow or the Cropping tool, choose Specifications from the Edit menu (or type Command-M) and a dialog box will appear in which you can resize the picture box or rescale the picture. You can resize a picture disproportionately, if you wish, by typing in different numbers for Scale Across and Scale Down.

Right: A 96 pt Century Italic *a*, scaled in a picture block to 100% x 200%, center, and 200% x 100%, far right.

Use the cropping tool like a hand tool to slide the picture around inside the block until its position is correct. The outside edges of the picture block will crop off any portion of the graphic hidden behind it; make the block larger if necessary.

Importing pictures To be able to bring an electronic art file into a picture block in a page layout program, you must first save the art file in a format that the program can read (see page 54). For MacPaint and SuperPaint documents, you need to open the illustration document in the program in which it was created, select Save As from the File menu, add "/pict" to the document name, click the button PICT, and click Save.

For Illustrator and other PostScript graphics applications, open the illustration file in the program in which it was created, select Save As from the File menu, add "/eps" (short for Encapsulated PostScript) to the document name, click Apple Macintosh Preview, and click Save.

If you know you have a picture on your disk, but it doesn't show up in the directory window when you go to Get Picture, it's probably not saved in the correct file format. Follow the steps above, and the picture should come in.

Using picture blocks to scale type If you want to scale headline type larger than the maximum point size available, or you want to warp it by scaling it disproportionately, you can do so by copying it into a picture block. First, select the text block (not the text itself) with the selection arrow. Type Command-C to copy it to the clipboard. Next, create a picture block and click in it with the Cropping tool, to prepare it to receive a picture. Type Command-V, and the image on the clipboard will be pasted into the picture block. You can now rescale the type in the picture's Specification dialog box. **NOTE:** The type is now a picture, and can no longer be edited with the I-beam tool. This trick is best used for heads, not text.

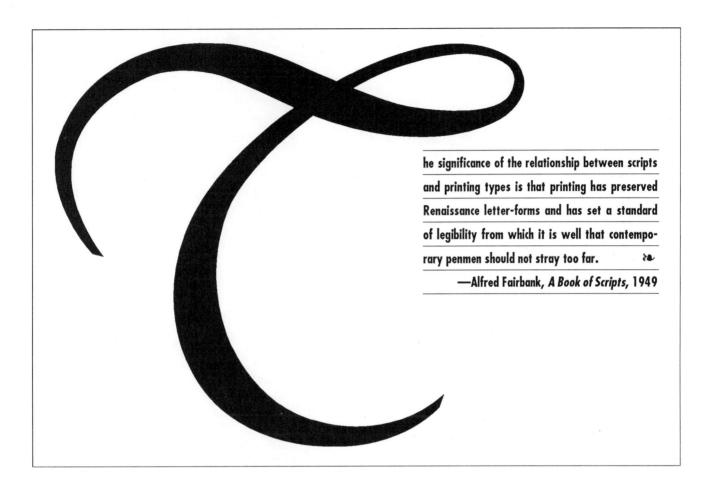

he significance of the relationship between scripts and printing types is that printing has preserved Renaissance letter-forms and has set a standard of legibility from which it is well that contemporary penmen should not stray too far.

—Alfred Fairbank, *A Book of Scripts*, 1949

Use RSG to make thumbnail sketches and rough layouts, like the design shown above. The script T was scanned on an Abaton scanner, saved as a MacPaint file, traced and refined in Adobe Illustrator, and saved as an EPS file for importation into a picture block in RSG. The text is all in one text block, both justified and, for the last line of type, flush right. Note that RSG justifies type by manipulating word spacing, not letter spacing, so it is most effective when there are sufficient words per line length to allow for adjustment between words. The rules were created by first making and positioning the top rule, then duplicating it six times with a horizontal offset of 0 picas and a vertical offset of .18 points, the same as the line spacing for the text.

It is important to turn off the Runaround feature in the Specifications dialog box for a picture block if you don't want any nearby text to be repelled from, or run around, a graphic image. In the design above, the text tucks in close to the graphic image of the script T, overlapping the picture block, so Runaround is turned off. You could also select Ignore Runaround in the Specifications dialog box for the text block. Runarounds are used when you want to wrap text around a picture block or the graphic shape inside a picture block, like the text run around menus on pages 70 and 71 of this book. You can specify an exact repel distance to two decimal points in the picture block Specifications dialog box.

This typographic
illustration was
created in RSG
by first creating
a text block,
typing in a lower-
case b at 150
percent, then
selecting the text
block with
the arrow tool,
copying it
to the Clipboard,
pasting it
into an activated
picture block,
and scaling the
block to
300% width by
700% depth.

disproportionate scaling: from a 150 point Bodoni b to a **300% wide** by 700% tall *stretch* b

The body text is
typed into two
text blocks, one
of which is filled
with black,
and the text is
colored white by
selecting Color
from the Text
menu. Both are
placed into
position and
aligned precisely
using the
Alignment dialog
box under the
Special menu.

Chapter 9: Fonts

When you work with type
on the Macintosh, you
work with typefaces that
are specially created
for use on the computer.
All typefaces must be
redrawn and saved in
electronic file formats
before you can use them
on the computer. All
computer typefaces are
either bit-mapped,
meaning they are made up
of pixels, or they are
object-oriented and made
up of a mathematical
description as is the
PostScript programming
language. To view any
typeface onscreen, you
need a screen font version
of the face, which is
bit-mapped. To print to a
PostScript printer, you also
need a printer font, or
PostScript file describing
the font.

Illustration by Max Seabaugh in Adobe Illustraor

MACINTOSH TYPE FONTS

When you work with type fonts on the Macintosh, you are actually working with two separate kinds of electronic files representing each type font.

Screen fonts

Screen fonts come with the font packages that you purchase from any of the companies that manufacture and sell type fonts for the Macintosh. They are installed directly into your System file—located inside the System folder—with a utility program called the Font/DA (Desk Accessory) Mover. The Font/DA Mover must be used to install screen fonts into the System file, since you cannot open or make changes to a System file in any other way.

Bitmaps or outlines
Screen fonts are either outlines of the fonts drawn with bezier curves which are filled in onscreen, or they are bit-mapped representations of fonts, drawn in various point sizes, especially for viewing onscreen at the screen resolution of 72 dpi.

Screen font point sizes
When you load a screen font into the System file, you should load several point sizes. Although the computer will scale missing point sizes up or down from the available installed sizes, the installed sizes look better onscreen than the scaled sizes.

Screen fonts can be made up of bit-mapped type that matches the screen resolution of 72 dots per inch.

However, the more point sizes of a font that are installed, the more space is taken up in memory. If you have installed a lot of fonts, you may run out of storage space. One trick to maximize the number of fonts you can fit into your System file is to install a limited number of screen font sizes for every font: we only install 10, 12, and 24 point sizes, for example. The Macintosh scales the in-between sizes for screen viewing, and although they look a little rougher onscreen, it doesn't affect print quality.

Printer fonts

The reason that print quality is not affected is that a separate electronic file is required to contain the data that downloads (sends a description of) the font to the output device. This file is called the printer font, also known as a downloadable font. It also comes with the font package that you purchase, but it is installed in the System folder, along with the System file, General, the Finder, and other files necessary to run the computer and peripheral devices. Only one file is necessary for all the point sizes of a font, since PostScript fonts are scalable. In some cases you may choose

Screen fonts may also be outline fonts. Made up of bezier curves, like a drawing in Adobe Illustrator, they appear onscreen in solid black, but actually print out as high-resolution bitmaps.

to buy a bit-mapped type font that prints pixelated; in this case its printer font will not be PostScript, but will be bit-mapped just like its screen font. Some people who only have dot-matrix printers choose to buy these fonts in lieu of PostScript fonts, which can't print optimally on bit-mapped printers.

Downloadable fonts
If you are doing quality design work, or are planning to output to a printer other than a Laser-Writer—such as a Linotronic or Compugraphic professional typesetting machine—you can purchase downloadable type fonts from a number of third-party developers. Adobe Systems, Inc., developer of the original PostScript programming language, has available an entire library of PostScript type fonts that were the first on the market, and are still considered the standard. You can find them at virtually every service bureau. Other fonts based on programming languages such as PostScript or TrueType are available from other manufacturers, but may or may not be

available at your service bureau. Apple itself is developing an alternate font format called TrueType that requires the not-yet available System Version 7.0 to run. Both should be available within the next year or so.

LaserWriter fonts

There is one exception to the rule that fonts are not installed in the printer itself. When you buy a laser printer, you can choose to buy one that already has a rudimentary selection of fonts installed in the printer that do not need to be downloaded in order to print. These usually include Times Roman, Helvetica Medium, Avant Garde, Palatino, Century Schoolbook, and a few others.

System-wide availability

Because screen and printer fonts are installed in the System file and System folder, it makes them available system-wide. This means that they are available from within any software application that you run on that system that has the ability to work with type.

Font substitution Downloadable fonts do not come with the software programs themselves, nor do they come with the output device; they are installed into a specific computer and are accessible from that computer.

If you print out your document from another computer, you must make sure that the same fonts are installed on that computer. If they are not, the Macintosh will substitute another typeface for the one that you specified—usually Geneva or Courier—with usually disastrous results on your design. This is called font substitution, and is why service bureaus always ask you for a list of fonts used in your file, as well as their manufacturer. To avoid font substitution they have to have exactly the same screen and printer fonts (with the same Font ID numbers) installed on the computer from which they'll be outputting your file.

Installing type fonts

To install a type font that you have purchased into your Macintosh requires two separate procedures. First you install the screen font into the System file using the Font/DA Mover, then you dump the printer font into the System Folder. The procedure for using the Font/DA Mover can be found in the Appendix at the back of this book (pages 91-95), and is also clearly outlined in every font package that you purchase.

Improving screen display

When the Macintosh screen display was first introduced, it was a vast improvement over previous computer screen displays that showed only the code representing a page, rather than the page itself. The term WYSIWYG (What You See Is What You Get—pronounced Wizzy-Wig) was coined to describe this revolutionary new screen display that actually let you see onscreen the work that you were creating.

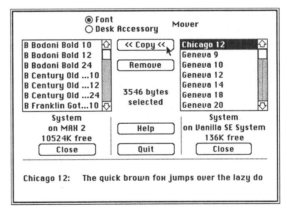

Chicago 12:   The quick brown fox jumps over the lazy do

Today WYSIWYG display looks crude and blocky, and computer users are insisting upon a quality of screen resolution that more closely matches that of the final output. Several improvements have been developed. A new kind of screen display called Display PostScript from Adobe Systems is currently

Left, an open dialog box is shown displaying the Font/DA Mover in action. The 12 point size of the screen font Chicago is being copied from the Vanilla SE System on the right, to the MAX 2 System on the left. You can select and copy more than one font at a time by shift-clicking. When only one font and size is selected at a time, a representation of that font is displayed at the bottom of the dialog box.

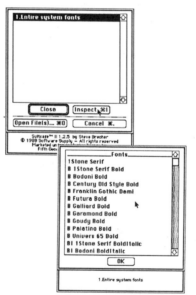

Font menus are getting longer, more confusing and more cumbersome, as shown above, top. Programs like Suitcase, Master Juggler, and Type Reunion (shown above, bottom) can help you manage your fonts and shorten your font menu.

available on the NeXT computer, and may soon be available on Macintoshes as well. Some Mac software applications such as LetraStudio, a display and headline manipulation program, use a technique called anti-aliasing, which takes advantage of the capabilities of the color monitor on a Mac II to soften, or blur, the edges of the pixels to make them look smoother. Adobe has also released a new product called Adobe Type Manager that you install into your System folder; it markedly improves the quality of screen display of type fonts as well as cuts down the number of screen fonts that must be installed into the System file.

Managing type fonts

One of the first problems you'll run into when your font library grows in size is font management. The more fonts you have, the larger your System file becomes, the more memory is used for font storage, and the longer your Font pull-down menus become.

Suitcase and Juggler There are several programs available that allow you to package fonts in smaller selection groups;

Suitcase and Master Juggler are examples. Suitcase (shown below) allows you to put fonts together in groups according to which fonts you usually use together, and package them in little "suitcases" that you can open and close from the Apple menu as a desk accessory.

Adobe Type Reunion and Type Manager Another brand-new program called Adobe Type Reunion allows you to install only one screen font from an entire font family, and then displays only the font family name in the Font pull-down menu. Font styles, such as roman, italic, bold, bold italic, etc., are accessed through pop-up menus to the side of each font name, thereby considerably shortening the overall length of your pull-down Font menus.

And, as already mentioned, Adobe Type Manager cuts down the number of screen fonts that must be installed into the System file.

Creating type fonts

Two fine programs are available that allow you to create your own PostScript type fonts: Fontographer from Altsys and FontStudio from Letraset. They work similarly to Adobe Illustrator, by describing letterforms as bezier curves, but they enable you to save your letterforms as fonts that are scalable and accessible from the Font menu, rather than as graphics files.

Manipulating type fonts

Several programs can enable you to manipulate type forms by stretching, skewing, slanting, scaling, or other special effects: LetraStudio from Letraset and Type Align from Adobe allow you to manipulate Adobe and other PostScript fonts, and Letraset also sells its own display fonts for use within LetraStudio. Also, both Adobe Illustrator and Aldus FreeHand enable you to manipulate letterforms to a certain degree and save them as graphics files.

Chapter 10: Printing

There are two kinds of output, or printing, that you will use on the computer. Proof printing is done as you work to fine-tune your design, and to show to your client, proofreader and editor to catch mistakes. Proof printing is usually done on the LaserWriter, a 300 dots-per-inch (dpi) PostScript printer that's inexpensive enough to have in your home or office, or on a low resolution color printer like the QMS for color comps. Typeset quality output is done on a high-resolution typesetting machine at your service bureau. Both machines use PostScript or other programming languages to describe and print your Macintosh files.

Illustration by Max Seabaugh in SuperPaint

MEDIUM-RESOLUTION PROOF PRINTING

An Apple LaserWriter PostScript printer

The Chooser dialog box shown below is found under the Apple menu. If more than one kind of printer is available to print to, its icon will appear in the directory at left. Choose the name of a specific printer in the directory at top right. Note that you can type in your own user name in the bottom field.

Printing on a LaserWriter

When you're ready to proof print a document on the 300 dpi LaserWriter, first open the file (if you haven't done so already). The document must be open onscreen before it can print.

Choose a printer Make sure that the printer you want to use is turned on and has printed out its test page. Then select Chooser from the Apple menu. The dialog box shown below will appear. Select the appropriate LaserWriter icon and make sure that it's highlighted (it might not look exactly like the LaserWriter icon shown here). When it is highlighted, the name or names of the available printer(s)—the printers that are hooked up to your computer via cabling and are turned on—should appear in the box titled Select a LaserWriter. Click to highlight the name of the printer you wish to print on.

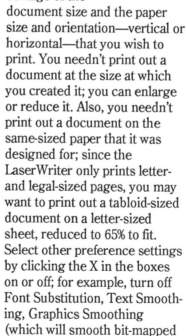

NOTE: If the LaserWriter icon does not appear or does not highlight when you click on it, check to make sure that it is turned on, that all the AppleTalk cabling between the printer and your computer is firmly connected, and that the correct printer resources—files named Laser Prep and LaserWriter— are installed in the System folder on your computer. You may need to consult your LaserWriter and/or Macintosh *User's Guide*.

Select page setup

Next, select Page Setup from the File menu and choose the percentage of the document size and the paper size and orientation—vertical or horizontal—that you wish to print. You needn't print out a document at the size at which you created it; you can enlarge or reduce it. Also, you needn't print out a document on the same-sized paper that it was designed for; since the LaserWriter only prints letter- and legal-sized pages, you may want to print out a tabloid-sized document on a letter-sized sheet, reduced to 65% to fit. Select other preference settings by clicking the X in the boxes on or off; for example, turn off Font Substitution, Text Smoothing, Graphics Smoothing (which will smooth bit-mapped

drawings if clicked on) and Faster Bitmap Printing (will bitmap rather than smooth any pixelated drawings or type fonts), and, under Options, turn on Larger Print Area (decreases the margin size) and Unlimited Downloadable Fonts (increases the number of downloadable fonts or other PostScript data that the printer will accept). Click OK to exit the dialog box, then type Command-S to save the settings you've just selected.

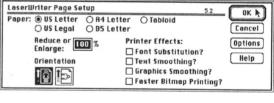

Select print Now select Print from the File menu. The blinking insertion bar will be in the first box; type in the number of copies you want to print of each page. Next, press the Tab key to jump to the next box and type in the starting page number and, in the last box, the ending page number of the pages you want to print (you must print consecutive pages). Or, if you want to print all the pages in the file, just click the button for All. Click OK.

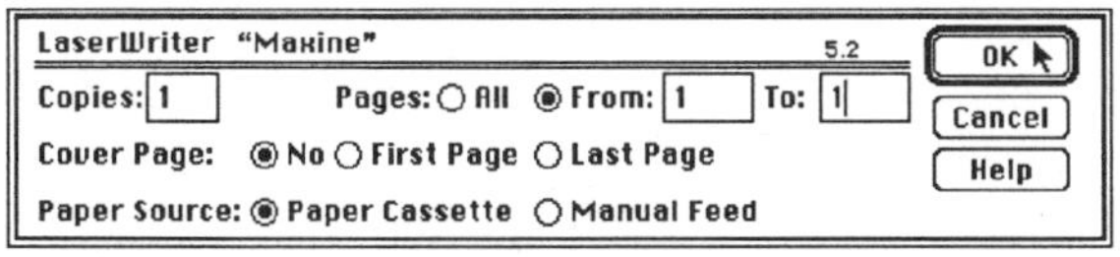

```
LaserWriter  "Maxine"                        5.2    [ OK ▸]
Copies: 1          Pages: ○ All  ● From: 1  To: 1   [Cancel]
Cover Page:  ● No ○ First Page ○ Last Page          [ Help ]
Paper Source: ● Paper Cassette  ○ Manual Feed
```

A handy shortcut: instead of positioning the I-beam tool inside each box (also called fields) individually, just press the Tab key and you'll jump from one box to another. This will only work with true fields—the square boxes—and not with buttons—the round circles—shown above. Use this trick when filling in the page numbers in the Print dialog box, for example, as shown above.

A series of dialog boxes will appear telling you the current status of the job: "looking for LaserWriter," "initializing printer," etc. You may have to wait in line behind another user; data is sent to the printer on a first-come, first-served basis. A dialog box will tell you the name of the user currently printing, and will tell you when it begins to send your file. It will take a few minutes for the data to be sent from the computer to the printer. Pay attention, however: occasionally a dialog box will appear briefly, asking you a question, telling you if the printer is out of paper or if a problem has been encountered during printing. You should be available to attend to these inquiries or messages before printing can continue.

Time and patience Using quality PostScript or other download-able type fonts results in far better word- and letter-spacing and letterforms than merely using the fonts that come with the printer. However, download-ing these fonts to the printer takes a lot of data—and time—and it is strongly recommended that you limit the number of fonts used in one document to a maximum of four or five

unless you turn on the Unlimited Downloadable Fonts selection under Options in the LaserWriter Page Setup dialog box. Also, printing graphics files such as scanned images or Encapsulated PostScript files can be extremely time-consuming because these files take up a lot of memory. Be patient.

Increasing printer speed Using one of the newer LaserWriters can speed up the amount of time it takes to output a file. Before you purchase a printer, compare features, the amounts of RAM, and output speeds; check the hardware reviews published by computer maga-zines like *Macworld*, *MacUser*, and *Publish* magazines.

If output time is a critical issue, you might want to consider buying a separate hard disk on which to load all your printer fonts, and attach it directly to your printer's SCSI (pro-nounced "scuzzy") port. It will speed up the printing process measurably.

Color proof printing

If you want to print out full-color proof prints at 300 dpi, you can use a QMS or other medium-resolution color PostScript output device. These are quite expensive, and rather than pur-chase one yourself, you'll proba-bly elect to send your files to a service bureau for output.

Send proper instructions When you send files to a service bureau for output, it always pays to send along complete instruc-tions regarding your file. Be sure to tell your service bureau the following things: what pro-gram you created the file in, what version number of the pro-gram you used, what type fonts you used and from what manu-facturer, what kind of computer you created the file on, and what versions of the System files you used. Also tell them whether you want your output on paper or film, letter- or tabloid-sized, what percentage size, and how many each of which page num-bers to print. Finally, include your proof-pages printed as a sample of how the final output should look.

What to avoid Small type and fine lines in color break apart at 300 dpi; large areas of solid colors, graphics, and illustra-tions will print best. Keep small type black or, if in color, keep it big. If your design contains small colored type, medium-resolution color proof printing won't be satisfactory. You may want to have your client view the work onscreen. You could also go directly to a color separa-tion and matchprint proof, or you might see if there is a higher resolution color printer in your area.

HIGH-RESOLUTION TYPESET OUTPUT

A high-resolution Linotronic PostScript type-setting machine

Remember that Illustrator's illustration board metaphor actually divides the image area into 9 segments, each of which prints out as a separate page, sequentially numbered from 1 to 9, left to right, top to bottom. Your image is usually in the center of the image area, or page 5: instruct the printer to print from page 5 to 5, not all pages.

Service bureaus

Unless you're wealthy enough to afford your own Linotronic or Compugraphic typesetting machine, printing on one of these machines probably means dealing with a service bureau— a typesetting or desktop publishing center with the ability to output Macintosh files.

Prepare your document Spend your time and money wisely by doing all your proof printing at your home or office, proofing and correcting your document until it's as perfect as you can make it. Any time you spend altering your files on the computer at the service bureau is time you'll have to pay for.

Prepare your disks When you're through preparing your document, copy the file and the application you used to create it —unless you're sure that the service bureau has not only the same application, but the same version of the application—onto a floppy disk to send to the service bureau. If you're sending a page layout program file that contains imported graphics files, put the graphics files into the same folder as the layout document. This speeds up printing time, because the computer doesn't have to search through the hierarchical filing system to find the graphics files.

Sample output and order forms

Next, print out a sample of your document on your proof printer to send along to the service bureau as a sample of what the document should look like when printed. Write the following information on the sample, or on the service bureau's order form:

1   The name of the file and the name of the disk on which it can be found
2   The page orientation: vertical or horizontal
3   The page size you want to print out on (not necessarily the same as the document page size): letter, tabloid, or other
4   The percentage at which it should print (100% or other)
5   The application name and version number in which the file was created (if you are not sending those along with the document)
6   The hardware configuration you worked on and the version numbers of the System file and LaserWriter and Laser Prep files installed on it
7   All of the type fonts and styles used in the file and by whom they were manufactured
8   Your name, address, phone number, job or purchase order number, return delivery method, and account number if appropriate

Printing problems

The better prepared your files, disks, order forms, and samples are, the better chance you'll have of your document printing successfully. However, problems do sometimes occur.

Compatibility Sometimes you'll run into problems printing on a high-resolution printer that didn't occur when you printed the same file on the proof printer in your office. Make sure to supply the service bureau with all the information they need so that they can be sure to print from the same version of the program, preferably on the same hardware configuration, and using the exact same screen and printer fonts that you used when you created your document. If you frequently have trouble printing, you might look for a service bureau that has more experience printing files from the program you used. They may be able to help solve the output problem.

Limit file size Frequently files print more smoothly if you limit the file to no more than about 12 pages each. Experiment to find a comfortable page number for the job you are doing and the program you are using. The smaller the file, the less time it takes to open, save changes, and close the file—as well as to print it. And remember to put any imported files into the same folder with the file in which they are used.

MECHANICAL OR SPOT COLOR SEPARATIONS

Mechanical separations

Color separations in drawing or painting programs like SuperPaint or MacPaint can be created mechanically by first creating base art, then duplicating the file and modifying it for each subsequent color printer, or overlay, as shown here. This type of color separation is the same as a traditional mechanical color separation created with different overlays of hand-cut rubylith, except in this case duplication and modification of the original file ensures exact alignment of each layer, and output consists of negative film from a high-resolution typesetting machine. The illustration above was drawn in SuperPaint, and represents a black outline that will be filled with spot, or mechanical, colors. The printer still strips in the process color screen tints, or the overlays can be used to print Pantone spot colors.

1 Create base art for the black printer (the subsequent layers of colors will be referred to as color printers or as overlays). Put a single pixel dot—or draw a true register mark with the circle and line tools—in the upper left-hand corner of the window to use to register the overlays with the original. The original, above, is saved, and then duplicates of the file are saved under alternate names (such as Blue Printer, Gray

Printer, Red Printer) and altered for each different layer of color.

2 Modify the duplicate files one by one. Use the selection marquee to select the entire image area. Reverse the image by selecting the Invert command. This will change all black linework to white, and fill in all white areas with solid black. Any areas filled with black are used as mechanical overlays to print a second color. Use the Paintcan tool filled with white to delete any areas filled with black that won't be used in this color printer. Whatever is left will print. Go back to the original base art each time you duplicate, rename, and modify a color layer.

3 Be sure to print out proof copies of your mechanical separations and view them on a light box to make sure that no one area is filled on two overlays, and that all areas that should be filled with a color appear on one of the overlays.

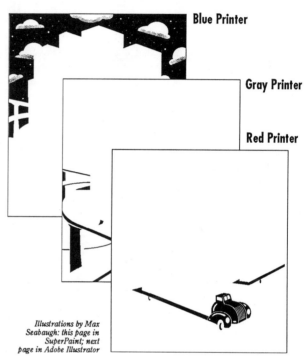

Blue Printer

Gray Printer

Red Printer

Illustrations by Max Seabaugh: this page in SuperPaint; next page in Adobe Illustrator

Check also to see that every color you are using has an overlay representing that color.

4 Print out all overlays on negative film on a high-resolution typesetting machine, and have matchprint proofs made to proof the separations.

Composite separations

You can also send your electronic files out to a Scitex color separation house and have four-color composite negative film separations created, and a matchprint proof made for color proofing.

Just like traditional mechanical color seps, each file represents a layer of color, a window into which solids and screen tints are stripped to create process or spot colors. Above, white highlights have been added to represent clouds in the Blue Printer and shine on the truck in the Red Printer, while the Gray Printer is a simple solid fill.

FULL COLOR SEPARATIONS

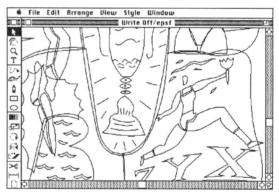

View your illustration onscreen in B&W or tints of black and use dialog boxes to fill in color selections in either process color values or Pantone colors. Proof on a B&W printer, which prints out black screen tints representing the color values you've selected, or in color on a QMS at your local service bureau.

Color in black and white

Specifying color onscreen doesn't necessarily require a color computer. Most drawing programs that support color—like Adobe Illustrator and Aldus FreeHand—can be used on a black and white computer. The only exceptions are pixelated color programs; because they require the extra differentiation of color to separate one pixel from the next, they can only be used on color computers with color screens.

Specifying process colors To

specify process colors for either the stroke and/or fill attributes of an illustration, type in percentage values for Cyan, Magenta, Yellow, and Black, referring to standard process color charts if necessary to view

the colors. For example, 100% Magenta and 100% Yellow would yield a bright, rich red, whereas 50% Cyan and 50% Magenta would yield violet. Any percentage from 0 to 100 can be specified for each of the four process colors.

Specifying Pantone colors In Aldus FreeHand, Pantone colors are available under the Fill and Stroke menus by color number, and these colors can be added to a short color menu for the document. In Adobe Illustrator, a special Pantone color file must be duplicated and opened instead of just creating a New file; that special file carries with it all the data needed to use Pantone colors.

When you start a new file based on this special Pantone colors file, the Paint dialog box will have both process and Pantone color choices available for both the stroke and fill attributes.

Output

Take your electronic file to a service bureau for output directly to negative film. Adobe Illustrator, for example, has a companion program called Adobe Separator that enables you to four-color or spot-color separate your file. The negative film can then be used to make match-print, chromalin, or color key proofs. If your service bureau isn't set up to make them, the film can be sent out to any standard color separation house.

The future Technology is currently available and/or being developed that will enable you to send electronic illustration and page layout files directly to a Scitex, Hell, or Crosfield color separation facility for full color separations and proofs. Quark XPress currently has full separation capabilities, and PageMaker and DesignStudio are not far behind. This is probably one of the most important areas to watch in this rapidly changing technology.

Appendix

This Appendix will help you make use of the mini-applications called Desk Accessories found under your Apple menu. The Control Panel DA lets you control user preferences such as mouse and keyboard speed, sound levels, desktop background patterns, and others. Find File helps locate documents lost in the maze of the hierarchical filing system. Key Caps lets you find and make use of all the hidden characters available in a type font. And Scrapbook lets you save, cut, and paste art images from one central storage place into your documents. Learn more about using the Font/DA Mover and about setting up your System folder, too.

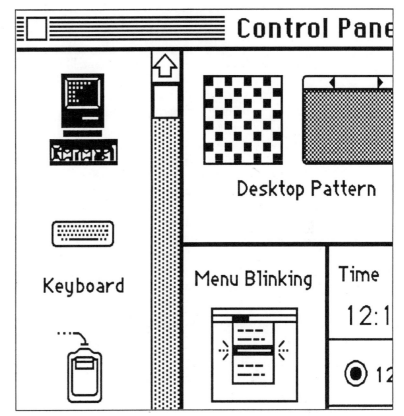

DESK ACCESSORIES

Desk accessories

Desk accessories (DAs) are mini-applications found under the Apple menu. They are small programs that provide a single function, like taking notes, setting an alarm, keeping a scrapbook of images, setting user preferences for your computer, or finding keyboard placement of characters in a font. Most importantly, they can be used while you are inside another application, without having to quit and return to the Desktop. Desk accessories are loaded into the System using the Font/DA Mover, just as you move type fonts.

The Control Panel The Control Panel is a desk accessory available in every System. It allows you to select a background screen pattern, the speed of the blinking insertion bar, the mouse speed, the loudness of the speaker volume, the date and time, and other user preferences.

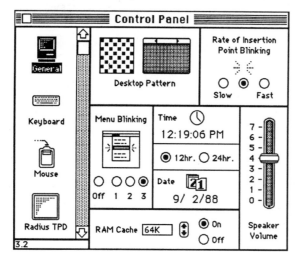

Eureka and Find File These files are desk accessories that find misplaced files and documents on either your hard disk or on floppy disks currently in a disk drive port. To use one of these, select it from the Apple menu, and enter the name—or even part of the name—of the file or document that you are looking for. Click on the Find (or running man) button. If the file is on the currently selected disk, a chart will appear that shows

where in the hierarchical file system the file is located. Close the dialog box, and go to the location indicated to find your file. If the file cannot be found on the current disk, eject it and insert another disk and repeat the search until you find the document.

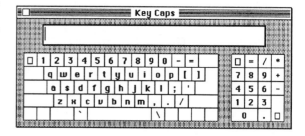

Key Caps Key Caps is a handy desk accessory that enables you to review the placement of font characters on the keyboard, including letterforms and symbols. Enter Key Caps by selecting it from the Apple menu. A dialog box will appear that displays the keyboard. At the far right-hand side of the menu bar, a new menu, Key Caps, will appear. Drag down the menu until you find the font that you want to look up, select it, and release the mouse button. The font characters will appear on the keyboard in the dialog box. Hold down the Option and Shift keys, or Option-Shift simultaneously, to see other character options available in that font.

To copy a character out of Key Caps Type the character into the space at the top of the dialog box by pressing its key on the keyboard. You can select the character typed in that box and cut and paste it into your document. If you've pasted it into a different font, you'll have to re-select the character from within your document and apply the font specification to the character before it displays properly. Click the Close box to exit.

UTILITIES

Scrapbook The Scrapbook is like a permanent version of the Clipboard. You can copy graphic or type elements to it, store them there, and paste them into other applications when needed.

To copy art into the Scrapbook First, open the document or file containing the art that you want to copy. Select the art with the selection arrow and type Command-C (Copy). Then open the Scrapbook on the Apple menu and type Command-V (Paste). The art will paste itself into the Scrapbook.

To paste art from the Scrapbook Open the document you want to paste the art into. Open the Scrapbook and scroll until you find the art you want to copy. Type Command-C (Copy) and close the dialog box. Then type Command-V (Paste) and the art will appear on your document page. (In some applications, you may need to prepare an active picture block first.) Move the art to the desired location and Save.

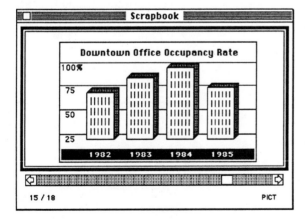

The Font/DA Mover Utility

This is a utility program that enables you to add type screen fonts and desk accessories to the System file. To use it, find and then double-click on the application icon (it may be in the folder labeled Utilities, or in the System folder, depending on how your HFS is set up).

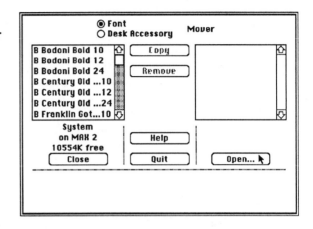

A dialog box (shown above) that contains two directories will open. One (shown on the left, above) will display a list of the type screen fonts in the System folder of the currently active startup disk. Insert a disk containing other screen fonts into the disk drive. Double-click on the Open button on the right side of the dialog box. (This button may sometimes say Close; don't worry—it's very confusing, but it's the right button!) A directory (see below) will appear in which you can find and open the System file of the second disk, or eject it and click on Drive to find a System file on another disk. When you open the second System file, the screen fonts it contains will be

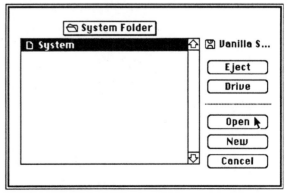

THE SYSTEM FOLDER

displayed in the right-hand directory in the Font/DA dialog box (see below). Select one or more fonts by highlighting them (shift-click to select more than one). The Copy button should turn black and point toward the left. If you press Copy while fonts are selected (as shown below), the application will copy them from the program in which they appear, into the program toward which the arrows in the Copy button are pointing.

The space underneath the directories tells you which system's font selections you are looking at in the directory window.

If only one font is selected, a sample appears at the bottom of the dialog box. (If more than one font is selected at a time, no sample will appear.)

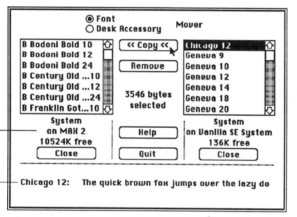

CAUTION: If you click Remove while a font is high-lighted, it will be removed from that disk. Be careful not to remove a font unless you are sure that you have another backup copy elsewhere.

To move desk accessories To move desk accessories from one System File to another, hold down the Option key while opening the Font/DA Mover, or, once open, click the Desk Accessory button at the top of the dialog box. Follow the same procedures for moving fonts, above.

TIP: To find the version number of any file, select its icon and type Command-I. A dialog box will appear that shows the version number of that file.

Installing printer fonts These are dropped directly into the System folder by selecting and dragging their names or icons from the disk they came on, and dropping them loose into the System folder. Do not put them inside any other folders inside the System folder, or the printer will not be able to locate them.

Font ID conflicts

Until recently, many programs identified type fonts by number rather than by name. This frequently caused font ID number conflicts, resulting in font substitution. Today most programs identify fonts by name, but if you are still having this problem when you send a job to a service bureau to print out on a typesetting machine, you might try sending along the System folder that you used to create the job, or use one of the font management applications like Suitcase, and send along a suitcase of the fonts that were used on the job. Keep a copy of a stripped system like the one below, with the bare minimum of files in it, to use when creating System folders for each new job or client, installing the screen and printer fonts of the typefaces that will be used.

The System Folder

A basic system is shown below, but you can also put together your own basic system. Use the Font/DA Mover to install the screen fonts of the type you want to include in the System file in this System folder. Then, at the Desktop level, dump the printer fonts for the fonts directly into the System folder, loose. It's a good idea to check with

Name	Size	Kind	Last Modified	
Vaccine	12K	document	Wed, May 25, 1988	11:40 AM
Appletalk ImageWriter	41K	document	Tue, Apr 14, 1987	12:00 PM
Backgrounder	5K	System document	Thu, Oct 8, 1987	12:00 PM
DA Handler	6K	document	Thu, Oct 8, 1987	12:00 PM
Easy Access	4K	document	Tue, Apr 14, 1987	12:00 PM
Finder	99K	System document	Thu, Jun 2, 1988	4:00 PM
General	14K	document	Thu, Oct 8, 1987	12:00 PM
ImageWriter	36K	document	Tue, Apr 14, 1987	12:00 PM
Key Layout	4K	document	Thu, Oct 8, 1987	12:00 PM
Keyboard	5K	document	Thu, Oct 8, 1987	12:00 PM
Laser Prep	25K	document	Thu, Oct 8, 1987	12:00 PM
LaserWriter	61K	document	Thu, Oct 8, 1987	12:00 PM
Mouse	4K	document	Thu, Oct 8, 1987	12:00 PM
PrintMonitor	33K	application	Thu, Oct 8, 1987	12:00 PM
Startup Device	3K	document	Thu, Oct 8, 1987	12:00 PM
System	223K	System document	Fri, Jun 3, 1988	1:06 PM

your service bureau to see what versions of the Macintosh System, Finder, and printer resources (the files named Laser Prep and LaserWriter) they use. Try to install and use the same version numbers if you can.

SHORTCUTS

Common Keyboard Shortcuts

The following is by no means a complete list of keyboard shortcuts. It does include most of the commonly *shared* shortcuts used in the programs discussed in this book. In cases where otherwise common shortcuts sometimes have different meanings, more than one definition may be included. Uncommon key commands unique to specific programs are not included in this chart.

Keyboard Command	Meaning	Programs in Which This Command Is Available
Command-A	Select All	DesignStudio, RSG, SuperPaint, Illustrator
Command-C	Copy	DesignStudio, RSG, MacWrite, SuperPaint, Illustrator
Command-D	Duplicate	DesignStudio, RSG, SuperPaint
Command-F	Find, or Find next	DesignStudio, RSG, MacWrite
Command-G	Group	DesignStudio, Illustrator
Command-I	Information	DesignStudio, RSG, the Desktop
	Paint dialog box	Illustrator
Command-N	New file	DesignStudio, RSG, SuperPaint, Illustrator
Command-O	Open file	DesignStudio, RSG, SuperPaint, Illustrator
Command-P	Print	DesignStudio, RSG, SuperPaint, Illustrator
Command-Q	Quit application	DesignStudio, RSG, SuperPaint, Illustrator
Command-S	Save	DesignStudio, RSG, SuperPaint, MacPaint, Illustrator
Command-T	Tabs	DesignStudio, RSG
	Type dialog box	Illustrator
Command-U	Ungroup	Illustrator
Command-V	Paste	DesignStudio, RSG, MacWrite, SuperPaint, Illustrator
Command-W	Close window	DesignStudio, RSG
Command-X	Cut	RSG, MacWrite, SuperPaint, Illustrator
Command-Z	Undo last command	RSG, MacWrite, SuperPaint, Illustrator

Index

R

S

Notes on Desktop Design
*An Introduction to the Use of
the Macintosh Computer as a Graphic
Design and Production Tool*

By Laura Lamar

Production Notes
This book was desktop published on a Macintosh
SE computer with a 40MB MacBottom
hard disk drive and a Radius TPD B&W monitor;
a Macintosh IIcx computer with a 40MB
internal hard disk drive and a Radius TPD full
color monitor, and an Apple Laserwriter Plus.

Software used includes Ready,Set,Go! 4.0
and 4.5a for writing and page makeup,
and Adobe type fonts Futura Bold Condensed
and Century Old Style. Cover, title page and
chapter dividers additionally use the type font
Matrix, designed by Zuzanna Licko of Emigré
Design, Emeryville, CA.

Cover art was produced using Aldus FreeHand,
Adobe Illustrator, and Ready,Set,Go!

Primary illustrations were drawn by Max
Seabaugh in SuperPaint, MacPaint and Adobe
Illustrator.

Indexing by Ira Kleinberg.